Harry S. Truman Little White House in Key West, Florida, circa 1949. *(U.S. Navy/Harry S. Truman Library)*

The Legacy
OF THE
Harry S. Truman
Little White House
Key West

Best Wishes

Bob Wolz

Presidents in Paradise

Robert Wolz and Barbara Hayo

www.historictours.com
www.trumanlittlewhitehouse.com

First Edition

Wolz, Robert and Hayo, Barbara.
    The Legacy of the Harry S. Truman Little White House Key West. - 1st ed.

ISBN 0-9752698-0-1
    1.Harry S. Truman - History. 2. Presidential Homes - History. 3. Presidents in Key West, FL - History. I. Title

Historic Tours of America.
The Nation's Storyteller.

Boston
Old Town Trolley Tours® • Ghosts & Gravestonessm
The Whites of Their Eyes • Boston Tea Party Ship & Museum

Key West
Old Town Trolley Tours® • Conch Tour Train • Harry S Truman Little White House
Key West Aquarium • Key West Shipwreck Historeum® • Mallory Square Festival Marketplace
Flagler Station Oversea Railway Historeum® • Schooner *Western Union* • Schooner *America*
Yankee Freedom Dry Tortugas National Park Ferry • Bone Island Shuttle

St. Augustine
Old Town Trolley Tours® • Ghosts & Gravestonessm • Old Jail
St. Augustine's Florida Heritage Museum • Beach Bus

San Diego
Old Town Trolley Tours • Ghosts & Gravestonessm• San Diego Seals
Old Town San Diego Market

Savannah
Old Town Trolley Tours® • Ghosts & Gravestonessm

Washington
Old Town Trolley Tours® • Monuments by Moonlight • DC Ducks

www.historictours.com

DEDICATION

As with President Truman, the most important things in my life are God and family and so this book is lovingly dedicated to my two sons, Jason Alexander and Grant Robert Wolz.

                    – Bob Wolz, Executive Director
                    Harry S. Truman Little White House

CONTENTS

ACKNOWLEDGEMENTS

For one hundred and thirteen years, several generations of national and international leaders have crossed the threshold of the Little White House in Key West, Florida, creating a story that has been waiting to be told. We are grateful to the many individuals, past and present, who have left us with intriguing pieces of information, which, woven together, make the story of this special place come alive.

The perseverance of Commander J.K. Winn, USN, in his requests for officers' quarters as early as 1883 led to the initial construction of the house, then known as Officers Quarters A & B. Local historians Ida Barron, Sharon Wells and Wright Langley fought to protect and preserve the Little White House and to have it listed on the National Register of Historic Places.

The meticulous logs of President Truman's official visits to Key West, kept by Commander William M. Rigdon, USN, provided insight into the daily presidential routine. The documents collected by Ava Moore Parks, preservationist and researcher for the creation of the Little White House Museum in 1989, were invaluable in the telling of the story.

Bob and Iris Bernreuter's gift of a collection of local newspapers, featuring all of President Truman's trips to Key West, gave us a great new primary source for research. Tom Hambright, Monroe County Library historian, graciously shared important details of Key West's military history and allowed access to the library's extensive collection of Key West history. The reading and research of Tom Marmion, retired history teacher and Little White House Museum tour guide, were extremely helpful in finding just the right source or quote. Little White House curator Bert Whitt's detailed knowledge of the house and its artifacts was invaluable.

Special thanks must go to Dr. Michael Devine, Pauline Testerman, Elizabeth Saffly, Mark Beveridge, Randy Sowell, and to the entire staff of the Harry S. Truman Presidential Library in Independence, Missouri, for their assistance in researching stories and quotations, and in identifying and reproducing countless photographs.

Finally, our gratitude goes to Ed Swift and Chris Belland, respectively President and CEO of Historic Tours of America, whose lifelong commitment to telling America's story has made this project possible.

Robert Wolz and Barbara Hayo

FOREWORD

Whenever anyone asks me about the Little White House in Key West, I always think of two things: the artichoke and the donkey. The artichoke was plunked down on my plate during what I think was my first visit, at a luncheon given for my grandfather, former President Harry S. Truman. It was in the spring of 1966 and I was nine years old. I'd never seen an artichoke before and I couldn't believe the grownups expected me to eat it. It looked like one of the palm trees outside, only more dangerous.

But that was nothing compared to the donkey.

From 1946 to 1952, my grandfather took 11 "working vacations" to the Little White House, the vacant commandant's quarters on what was then an active submarine base. The visits lasted anywhere from a few days to a few weeks and the pace was relaxed. Grandpa and his staff worked, but left plenty of time for swimming, napping, sipping bourbon and playing poker.

Grandpa especially liked to swim, often as a prelude to the napping, bourbon and poker. Near the Little White House, the story goes, there was no natural beach, so engineers trucked in sand and dumped it where the lawn dropped off to the water. They added a little cabana where he could change into his trunks.

One morning, according to the late *New York Times* photographer George Tames, Grandpa walked out with his trunks and towel over his arm, threw open the door to the cabana and got the shock of his life. There, standing in the presidential changing room, was a donkey, braying at him. Not only that, but it had answered the call of nature several times so the atmosphere in the cabana was rank, to say the least.

Grandpa stood, stunned, for a couple of seconds and then burst out laughing. After all, this was a man who had spent a dozen years as a farmer, so even if he didn't see donkeys in his cabana every day, he knew not to feel threatened.

The base commander was not nearly so amused. He initiated a search for the culprits and might have keelhauled them had Grandpa not intervened. As it turned out, they were a couple of reporters who got a little tipsy in town the night before, bought the donkey and smuggled it onto the base in the back of a taxi. You couldn't do that kind of thing today. The donkey would be found, x-rayed, given the once over by bomb-sniffing dogs, then sent to an underground holding facility in the Rockies, perhaps for years.

But Grandpa's reaction to the prank says a lot, both about him and Key West. In many ways, they were ideally suited to each other – straightforward and sure of themselves, but unpretentious and possessed of a sense of humor. Both enjoyed – and enjoy – an affinity for and acceptance of their fellow man. In Key West, Grandpa could be himself, let his hair down, wear a loud Hawaiian shirt or even grow a beard (which he started but never finished). He was delighted to have found the perfect haven from the pressures and posturing of a hectic world.

If he'd felt much more strongly about it, the face of American government might have been forever altered. After all, he's the one who once said: "I've a notion to move the capital to Key West and just stay."

–Clifton Truman Daniel

Harry S. Truman discovered the congenial ambiance of the Little White House in Key West, Florida.

President Harry S. Truman relaxing on the Little White House lawns on December 15, 1949, with Clark Clifford, special counsel to the president. *(U.S. Navy/Harry S. Truman Library)*

Its legacy continues as a venue for ongoing diplomatic efforts.

Secretary of State Colin Powell meeting with President Heydar Aliyev of Azerbaijan on the Little White House lawn on April 6, 2001. *(Andy Newman/Little White House Museum Collection)*

INTRODUCTION

On April 2, 2001, the Organization for Security and Cooperation in Europe, along with the U.S. Department of State under the leadership of Secretary of State Colin Powell, opened a week-long international peace summit between Armenia and Azerbaijan at the historic Harry S. Truman Little White House in Key West, Florida. Both countries have a history of territorial disputes dating back a millennium.

Why was Key West, better known for its Duval Street frolics, living coral reef and fishing, selected for this historic meeting? The State Department recognized what many did not: that this simple house on this small tropical island is imbued with a history of hosting meetings of international importance and has an inexplicable quality of being a setting where historic solutions are found.

Prior to the meeting of these two countries, this point was brought home in an observation made by a member of the Azerbaijan advance team as he walked through the Little White House the day before the talks opened. He was especially intrigued by the photographic exhibit of world leaders and statesmen who had once visited or used the Little White House: United States' Presidents Truman, Eisenhower, Kennedy and Carter, Britain's Prime Minister Harold Macmillan and King Hussein I of Jordan, to name a few. His comment to Robert Wolz, Little White House Executive Director, "You must be very proud of this place, it is so full of history," intuitively acknowledged that the Little White House, once the vacation retreat of President Harry S. Truman, is indeed a special historic place.

The relaxed, congenial atmosphere President Truman found in the home and on the island of Key West, so conducive to compromise, was the beginning of a legacy that continues into the present.

CHAPTER ONE

The Sentinel of the Straits
A short history of the United States military in Key West
"It is to the Gulf of Mexico what Gibraltar is to the Mediterranean."[1]
—Commodore David Porter, 1829

It was by chance, and reportedly also by design, that the modest home of a naval base commandant on a relatively obscure small island became a presidential retreat. The answer to how this came to be lies in the historic linkage between the strategic location of Key West and the presence of the United States Navy on the island.

Geographically, Key West lies like a sentinel of the Straits of Florida, the 110 mile shipping lane between Florida and Cuba. Since the days of exploration, ships running the Gulf Stream have had to navigate this narrow gauntlet.

The first people to the island of Key West came and went. Indians, explorers, Bahamians, Spanish and Cuban sailors, and others plying the trade routes found safe anchorage in its deep natural harbor, protected from storms by shallows and reefs. And they found fresh water on land and plentiful sea life in the near shore waters and surrounding reefs.[2]

When the territory of Florida was purchased by the United States from Spain in 1819, the ownership of Key West came immediately into question. Was this small, strategically located island, with its protected deep harbor, lying closer to Cuba than to the mainland of Florida, a part of Cuba? Was it the westernmost island of the Bahamian island chain, thereby placing it under British rule? Or was it a part of Florida, some 150 miles away, and now an American territory?

This issue was settled on March 25, 1822, when Navy Lieutenant Matthew C. Perry, commander of the schooner *Shark*, sailed into Key West harbor and raised the American flag. With this act, the United States took possession of the island. Shortly thereafter, Key West was declared an American port of entry.[3]

Key West 1820s to late 1860s
The Anti-piracy Squadron, wrecking industry and Union port

Pirates had long antagonized American shipping in the Straits of Florida and in the Gulf of Mexico, using the nearby Caribbean islands as a base of operations. In 1823, the Navy sent Commodore David Porter to establish a naval base in Key West to serve as headquarters for the West Indian Anti-piracy Squadron. This early base consisted of a storehouse, workshop, hospital and quarters for the men.[4]

The West Indian Anti-piracy Squadron, given the name, "Mosquito Fleet," consisted of a variety of shallow draft craft, providing Commodore Porter the ability to pursue and attack pirates hiding in shallow water. *(National Archives/Monroe County Public Library Archives)*

Commodore David Porter, USN, established the first naval presence in Key West in 1823. *(National Archives/Monroe County Public Library)*

As early as 1829, the importance of the location of Key West was acknowledged by Porter in a letter in which he informed the Navy that "the harbor of Key West, in my opinion, is the best harbor within the limits of the United States or its territories to the south of the Chesapeake."[5] In waging war against approximately two thousand "Brethren of the Coast,"[6] he clearly understood that all trade, going north and south, or to the west, had to sail through the Straits of Florida, the 110 miles between Key West and Cuba.[7]

Although Porter's naval campaign against the pirates was successful, devastating outbreaks of yellow fever in 1826 led to the closing of the Key West Naval Station.

Military presence returned to Key West in February 1831 with the arrival of Major James Glassel and two infantry companies to establish a ten-acre army garrison in the northeastern section of the island.[8] The bay, or bight, adjacent to the location of the base became known as Garrison Bight, a name it still bears today.

The strategic location of Key West was recognized by the United States government in 1836 when it was selected by Congress as one of the locations for a series of forts to be built along the coastline, from Maine to the Washington Territory. These forts were intended to defend the perimeter of the United States and its territories against foreign attack.

Fort Zachary Taylor and the East and West Martello Towers in Key West, and Fort Jefferson, located on a small island 70 miles west of Key West, were built as a result of this coastal defense effort. Construction on the forts began in 1846 and continued into the Civil War. The invention of the rifled cannon during the Civil War made these brick fortresses obsolete.[9]

By 1854, Key West was growing rapidly, becoming, for a time, the wealthiest city per capita in the United States. This growth spurt and subsequent wealth were brought about by the role the island played in the wrecking, or ship salvaging, industry. Merchant ships traveling the Gulf Stream through the Florida Straits frequently veered, or were blown, off course and ran aground on the jagged coral of the unmarked reefs paralleling the shipping lanes. Key West was the closest deep harbor port to the groundings on the reefs, placing the small island city at the epicenter of the wrecking industry. It was here that courts convened to settle the inevitable disputes that arose out of claims of ownership, salvage rights, and division of valuable cargo.[10]

Ft. Taylor

Sketch of Key West circa 1855 by James C. Clapp illustrates the island's rapid economic growth prior to the Civil War. Its population of 2,700 prospered from the vast wealth awarded from ship salvaging and from the many shipping-related businesses resulting from the port activity. The 3-story Fort Zachary Taylor, in the center background of the sketch, guards the harbor. *(Historic Tours of America®)*

In response to the need to provide protection for this flurry of maritime activity, the Naval Station in Key West was re-established in January 1854. At this time the Navy made the $10,400 purchase of the 2.7-acre tract of land upon which Officers Quarters A & B would later be built.[11] Just short of one hundred years after the land purchase, those quarters would be transformed into the Little White House.

The Civil War found Key West in an unusual situation: it was a Union port in a Confederate state. On January 10, 1861, Florida delegates had voted to secede from the Union, thus siding with the Confederacy. However, at this same time, there was a contingent of the U.S. Army stationed at Garrison Bight in Key West. Three days after Florida declared itself a Confederate state, Captain John Brannan, U.S. Army, without the knowledge of the town's Confederate sympathizers, marched his soldiers from their barracks on the northeastern side of the island to Fort Zachary Taylor on the southwestern side of the island. He held the fort until reinforcements could arrive, thus securing Key West as a Union port.[12]

Key West during the Civil War years. Engraving in *Harpers Weekly* shows Fort Zachary Taylor in the foreground, flying the Union flag. *(U.S. Navy/Little White House Museum)*

Both the Union army and navy used Key West as an active base during the Civil War. In addition to the ships, nine hundred soldiers were stationed in Key West and two hundred more at Fort Jefferson. These troops consisted of the 90th New York Infantry, the 47th Pennsylvania Infantry, the 2nd U.S. Colored Infantry, and various detachments. One hundred ninety-nine suspected Confederate blockade runners, captured by the Key West based Eastern Gulf Blockade Squadron, were brought to Key West, where they were held.[13]

The importance of Key West's location was clearly recognized by the Union as "more ships were stationed in Key West than at any other port in the United States, and but for its occupancy by the Northern forces as a naval base, the result of the war might have been different."[14]

While there were no hostile shots by the Confederates upon Key West, there were casualties nonetheless. Over three hundred soldiers and their dependents, and an unknown number of sailors, died from yellow fever epidemics in 1862, 1864 and 1865, as well as from accidental explosions.[15]

At the end of the Civil War, the army base became inactive; the naval station was again reduced to a supply depot and repair facility.

Key West 1870s to 1890s
Buildup to the Spanish American War

In the 1870s, the limited military presence in Key West grew in direct response to tensions with Spain over the ongoing revolutionary unrest in Cuba that had shattered the peace on that island for over forty years. The proximity of the Key West harbor to Cuba made it a natural staging area for these naval operations. "In 1873, when the capture of the *Virginius* threatened war with Spain, nearly every available ship in the Navy was hurried to Key West, which made it the base of all operations."[16]

The Atlantic Fleet (in background) gathering in Key West in response to the *Virginius* capture. Sketch, circa 1873, is from West Martello looking towards Fort Taylor. *(National Archives/Langley Collection)*

There was more than being the site of a U. S. Naval base that connected Key West to Cuba. Key West's proximity to Cuba had naturally and historically led to the flow of people and goods moving between the two islands, establishing strong familial bonds and business relationships between the two peoples. Over time, the conditions brought about by the revolution led to an increase in migration of Cubans to Key West. By the 1880s, approximately half of Key West's population of 20,000 was of Cuban descent, and the people of the island city provided considerable aid and shelter to the Cuban revolutionaries.[17]

Although tensions with Spain subsided to some degree after the *Virginius* incident, issues remained unresolved. The importance of Key West to naval operations in the region and the need to maintain the buildup of the base were expressed as far back as 1883 by the "very sensible views and suggestions" of Lieutenant Commander J.K. Winn, USN, the "energetic and efficient Commander of that depot."[18]

In a letter written to Captain A. W. Johnson, USN, dated May 1883 and forwarded to Rear Admiral E. F. Nichols, USN, Chief of Bureau of Yards and Docks, Commander Winn cited his years of service at the naval station in Key West to justify his being in a "position to know its needs and its importance to the Navy in particular, and the United States in general."[19] He looked to Key West's role in the future by emphasizing "its excellent harbor, or how easily it can be defended, its close proximity to the West Indies and South America makes it the natural rendezvous and base for Military or Naval operations in the case the Isthmus Canal is finished, American interest must have control of it, and there is no doubt that a large fleet will have to occupy these waters."[20]

In the same letter, in addition to stressing the importance of Key West's location, Winn cited the need for officers' housing. Some seven years later, in 1890, the Navy acted upon this request by beginning construction on Officers Quarters A & B. Prophetically, his prediction of the future importance of the Key West Naval Station was realized in 1897, when, "on the breaking out of war with Spain, every available naval vessel was again sent to Key West, and the *Oregon* and *Marietta* made their record run from California to the all-important Key West."[21]

On January 24, 1898, the USS *Maine* sailed from Key West to Havana to protect the lives of American citizens living in Cuba who were threatened by riots related to the continuing effort of the Cuban people to free themselves from Spanish rule.

The USS *Maine* was stationed in Key West for several years before sailing to Havana in January 1898. While moored in Havana harbor on February 15, 1898, a mysterious explosion caused the *Maine* to sink, sparking the Spanish American War. *(Monroe County Public Library)*

The federal inquiry into the *Maine's* sinking was held in Key West at the Custom House. Rousing newspaper headlines, "Remember the *Maine*," focused national attention on Key West.[22]
(From l to r) Capt. French Chadwick, president of the inquiry, Capt. William Sampson, Lt. Cmdr. William Porter, and two unidentified civilians. Lt. Cmdr. Adolph Marix is in the foreground. Their conclusion pointed to a Spanish mine as the cause. Current consensus suggests the cause was a fire on board. *(National Archives/ Key West Art & Historical Society)*

"Two months later, on April 23, 1898, the first shot of the Spanish American War was fired from the USS *Nashville* across the bow of the Spanish steamer *Buena Ventura* just a half mile off Key West."[23] During this brief international conflict, Key West was a major Navy port, supplying naval vessels and personnel.

At the close of the nineteenth century, Key West was the site of the only naval base south of Port Royal, South Carolina, and served briefly as the homeport of the entire Atlantic fleet.[24]

Key West early 1900s
Headquarters for Caribbean naval communications

In 1906, three 150-foot wooden masts were erected for the Navy in Key West by the American DeForest Wireless Telegraph Company as components of a new naval communications station. This communications facility positioned the Key West Naval Station to become the headquarters for Caribbean naval communications, with additional radio stations established in Puerto Rico, Cuba, Panama and Pensacola, Florida. Key West was now an important naval facility.

In 1906, wooden masts surround Officers Quarters A & B, which was completed in the summer of 1890. Radio antennas were placed on top of the masts. The power station that supplied electricity to the new station was housed next door in Building 21,[25] now national headquarters for Historic Tours of America®. *(Little White House Museum)*

Custom House

Building 21

Quarters A

The Navy replaced the earlier wooden communication towers with steel towers, dominating the low-scaled Key West skyline. *(Monroe County Public Library)*

A key component of this and future base expansions was the effort to control and expand the harbor and other coastline areas of Key West. An early attempt was made in 1882 with the construction of a 572 foot-long seawall under the direction of a young civil engineer, Lieutenant Robert E. Peary, of later Artic exploration fame.[26] This seawall ran directly in front of the site on which construction would later begin for the badly needed officers' quarters. In his 1883 correspondence, the forward-thinking Captain Winn also recommended such "concrete bulkheads be built in order to properly preserve these lands."[27]

Besides the need to control erosion, the increased construction taking place on the expanding naval facility from the early 1900s well into the 1960s demanded more land. To that end, there would be many efforts to expand the landmass of Key West by building seawalls and backfilling them through dredging.

Custom House

John Geiger House
(today the Audubon House)

Building 21

Quarters A & B
(today the Little White House)

U. S NAVAL STATION KEY WEST, FLA.
Contract 1819   DREDGING ETC.
General View.   August 1-09

In 1909, the Navy greatly increased the land in front of Quarters A & B and Building 21, expanding it well beyond the seawall built by Lt. Peary some twenty-seven years earlier. Here, the seawall is in place, but the area is yet to be filled in. The dredging provided a deeper harbor to accommodate larger Navy vessels. *(National Archives/Little White House Museum)*

Key West 1914 – World War I Buildup
The Seventh Naval District, the Submarine Base and the Naval Air Station

With World War I looming in 1914, the Key West Naval Station became the head-quarters for the Seventh Naval District, with overall command of naval forces in Florida. Two years later, "when u-boats were reported in U.S. waters, the remaining available U.S. submarines – E2, the new Ns, and the four Ks, transferred from Hawaii, to the Caribbean, basing out of New London, Key West and other east coast ports."[28] The Key West Naval Station was now home to an important submarine base.

World War I Navy sub at the dock created by the 1909 dredging and filling. Location is behind the Custom House, where recreational cruise ships now dock. *(Monroe County Public Library)*

The Naval base was further expanded in June 1918 with the addition of the Naval Air Station. Established to train seaplane and blimp pilots, its first commanding officer was Coast Guard Lieutenant Stanley Parker. It was Lieutenant Parker who, on September 22, 1917, piloted the first naval flight in Key West aboard a Curtiss N-9 seaplane.[29] Approximately 500 naval aviators trained in Key West during World War I. By 1919, 989 enlisted men and 45 officers were stationed at the Key West Naval Air Station. These men were involved in training and in patrolling the Straits of Florida against German submarines sailing in the Gulf of Mexico.[30]

(Above) World War I seaplanes at Trumbo Point Naval Air Station, built on largely filled land leased from the Florida East Coast Railway. The Air Station consisted of a large blimp hanger, seven seaplane hangers, three seaplane ramps, barracks, repair shops and mess halls. (Below) Blimps were used to spot submarines. *(National Archives/Monroe County Public Library)*

Key West 1932
Naval Station deactivation and the Great Depression

The end of World War I brought about yet another contraction in the military presence in Key West. With the exception of the radio station, the Key West Naval Station was deactivated in 1932 and was left with a crew of less than a dozen men kept on as caretakers. Quarters A suffered the same fate as all other Navy properties and was closed.

Other devastating events followed on the heels of the base closure. The final stage of the relocation of the cigar industry from Key West to Tampa, the sponge blight, and the Depression brought the Key West economy to a halt. Cumulatively, these factors were catastrophic to the economy of Key West, resulting in the bankrupt city surrendering its charter to the state and federal governments. Over eight thousand citizens left Key West during 1932-33. Eighty percent of those who stayed were on relief, and the entire city of Key West became a project of the Federal Emergency Relief Administration.[31]

Key West 1938
World War II Buildup

Faced with war in Europe, President Franklin Roosevelt declared a state of national emergency in September 1938. As a result, the Key West Naval Station was reactivated and a buildup ensued. The combination of strategic location and threat of war once again gave Key West new life.

The war across the Atlantic came close to home as German submarines prowled threateningly close to the east coast of the United States. Attacks off the coast of Florida reached a peak in 1942, with 102 allied ships severely damaged or sunk. Several, the *Santiago de Cuba*, the *Manzanillo*, the *Managus*, and the *Gulfstate*, as well as one German U boat, were sunk within 50 miles of Key West.[32] The newly opened East Coast Sound School, later known as the Fleet Sonar School, was established on the naval base in Key West to train against German submarine attacks.

During the war years of 1941 to 1945, the naval facilities in Key West reached their peak, expanding to enormous proportions, over 50 times in size, from 50 acres to 3200 acres. Over 15,000 sailors were assigned to duty here, as well as 3,400 civil service personnel. The convoy control center routed 8,000 ships, and the sonar school trained over 18,000 operators to detect and track submarines.[33]

Key West harbor during World War II at the time of heightened naval activity. *(Monroe County Public Library)*

The base was alive with activity. Much that had been closed and boarded up at the conclusion of World War I was reopened and refurbished, including Quarters A, this time as the home of the submarine base commander.

Series of postcards of the Key West naval base at its height during World War II *(Colour Pictures Publications/Little White House Museum)*

MAIN ENTRANCE TO U. S. NAVAL STATION, KEY WEST, FLORIDA

Ship's Store

Recreation Room

US NAVAL OPERATING BASE

KEY WEST, FLORIDA

Officer's Row, Naval Air Station

Officer's Row, Naval Operating Base.

Administration Building on Section Base.

Administration Building, Naval Operating Base.

ADMINISTRATION
BARRACKS &
HOUSING

BOCA CHICA FIELD

MEACHAM FIELD

NAVAL HOSPITAL

SALT POND KEY (ARMY)

REST BEACH NAVY HOUSING

NAVY COMMISSARY AND HOUSING

FORT TAYLOR (NAVY)

FORT TAYLOR (ARMY)

4 MILES

2.6 MILES

HARBOR DEFENSE (ARMY)

SEA PLANE BASE

RECEIVING STA.

SUBMARINE BASE

DREDGES KEY (NAVY)

NAVAL MAGAZINE

NAVY FUEL DEPOT

DEVELOPMENT STATION

MARINE RAILWAY-2 (NAVY)

Key West aerial map circa 1945-1948, showing extent of U.S. Navy operations on the island. (*U.S. Navy/ Harry S. Truman Library*)

31

The reopening of the base was a welcome event for the people of Key West. By providing thousands of jobs, it put them back to work. The impact on Key West of the phenomenal growth and activity of the naval base during World War II was emphatically expressed in a resolution adopted by the Key West Rotary Club in 1946, commending the base commander, Captain C. E. Reordan, USN, for "building and improving the Naval Operating Base."[34]

The commendation recognized that during the command of Captain Reordan, the first commander of both the air station and the submarine base, "the functions of said installations have increased to such an extent that they are now among the largest and most important installations of their kind operated by the Navy." The activity of the base was particularly high "during the month of November, 1944, which month represented the largest volume in the operational load placed upon the Base, the total of 1719 Naval vessels entered Key West in addition to merchant ships in convoy." [35]

The Navy's contribution to the local economy was not underestimated, nor did it go unappreciated. The Rotarians credited the base expansion under Captain Reordan with providing employment to local civilians "to the extent of $27,373,000.00," and honored his services for being "of inestimable value to the community of Key West, Florida."[36]

April 12, 1945
Franklin Roosevelt dies

President Franklin D. Roosevelt was re-elected for a fourth term in 1944 by a substantial margin over Thomas E. Dewey. On April 12, 1945, only months after his inauguration and less than a month before the war in Europe ended, President Roosevelt died of a cerebral hemorrhage. As the world mourned Roosevelt, Vice President Harry S. Truman assumed the presidency of the United States.

Reprinted with permission, Miami Herald Publishing Company

Key West 1946
President Truman discovers Key West

In 1946, after the conclusion of World War II, President Harry S. Truman had just completed his first nineteen months in office. The decision to drop the atomic bomb, the daunting task of rebuilding Europe and Japan, and the conversion of the U.S. from wartime production back to a peacetime economy had taken their toll on the Chief Executive. His personal physician, Brig. General Wallace Graham, MD, ordered him to take a vacation with plenty of rest in a warm climate.[37]

It may have been more by design than by accident that Key West was suggested as a possible vacation spot for the president. It was speculated that the possible motivation behind the suggestion by Fleet Admiral Chester Nimitz, USN, for the president to vacation in Key West was to showcase the Navy.[38]

In an article dated December 7, 1947, *The Miami Herald*'s Key West correspondent, Earl Adams, supported this notion: "A former Army man, Mr. Truman had to be made acquainted with the Navy and what better place than at Key West. Here he could see what the other team was doing." Adams explained the rationale behind this thinking: "The Navy bigwigs might deny it, but they were anxious for Mr. Truman to visit Key West. Aside from the fact that they knew he would find quietness and relaxation here they wanted him to get an insight into what the Navy was doing. They knew he would obtain that view here, for Key West is one of the Navy's most important developmental and experimental stations."

Whatever the intent, the stage was set for Key West to receive the President of the United States. He arrived on November 17, 1946, for the first of his 11 presidential visits to the island, residing in Quarters A, recently vacated by the base commander. Over the course of the presidential visits, Quarters A transitioned into the Little White House.

Throughout the years President Truman visited Key West, the last time as president being in March 1952, Cold War tensions kept the Key West Naval Station active. It became the largest anti-submarine training center on the East Coast. Anti-submarine aircraft squadrons at the air station included helicopters, blimps, seaplanes, carrier aircraft and patrol planes. This, combined with submarines, sub tenders and destroyers assigned to Key West, meant training could be conducted on the ocean's surface, underwater, and in the air.

The Advanced Underwater Weapons School trained naval personnel to maintain and operate anti-submarine weapons. The Underwater Swimmers School conducted courses in Scuba diving. The Naval Ordinance Unit provided for the testing of underwater explosives.

Sonar School graduation ceremony in 1949. The Fleet Sonar School trained more than 3,000 sonar operators each year and also trained a number of our allies.[39] *(U.S. Navy/ Harry S. Truman Library)*

(Left) President Truman presenting diplomas to graduates of the Fleet Sonar School in Key West on March 18, 1949. *(U.S. Navy/Harry S. Truman Library)*

(Right) President Truman climbing aboard a blimp in Key West in 1949. *(AP/World Wide Photos/Harry S. Truman Library)*

Late 1960s
Changing times lead to base closing

The changing times and changing technology of the late 1960s took their toll on the small island city. New military equipment and technological advances minimized Key West's usefulness in the new military strategy. Functional obsolescence, the diffusion of the Cuban missile crisis, and the shifting focus of the United States' foreign policy away from the western hemisphere turned the spotlight from Key West.

By March 1974 much of the naval station was de-established, including the Little White House, which, following the decision of President Truman in 1952 not to seek office, had returned to being the residence of the base commandant.

As a result of this closure, the Little White House and the surrounding homes and buildings used by the Navy remained vacant, gradually deteriorating.

Even the sign, designating the area as "Harry S. Truman Annex," was removed in April 1974. The sign, honoring President Truman, had been erected just two years earlier. *(Monroe County Public Library)*

Permission to use the name Harry S. Truman Annex for the area surrounding the Little White House had been requested by the city of Key West and was granted by Mrs. Truman following the death of the president on December 26, 1972. Today, the restored residential area once again bears the name. As it was in 1972, the name was adopted "as being most appropriate…since it is the setting of what must have been many fond memories for President and Mrs. Truman and the site of what is known as the 'Little White House.'"[40]

In 1986, some 12 years after de-establishment, the large parcel of abandoned Navy property, which included the Little White House, was sold at auction. The new owners, along with the federal government and the state of Florida, recognized the historic importance of the Little White House and began developing a plan for its restoration and preservation.

Key West 2004
The current presence of the Navy

The current focus of the naval base, now known as Naval Air Station Key West, is air defense related. Much of the port that sustained so much activity throughout the course of the history of the Navy in Key West has been transferred to the city of Key West.

The Navy, however, has retained the use of one of the piers facing the harbor. On many days, U. S. and allied naval vessels can be seen at the pier, in line with recreational cruise ships. In the words of the Naval Air Station commander, Captain Lawrence S. Cotton, USN, written expressly for this publication, Navy vessels, "from mine-hunters to cruisers, use the port for training, rest and recreation and emergency repairs."[41]

The naval facilities in Key West, according to Captain Cotton, "remain critical to the ability of military aviation and ship crews to train for and ensure the security of the United States." While there are no permanent air squadrons located in Key West, Boca Chica Airfield is "the location of choice for air to air combat training and is critical to the United States Atlantic Fleet in preparing Navy Battle Groups and Expeditionary Groups to deploy to the world's hotspots ready for combat."[42]

Captain Cotton's contemporary view that "Key West's location on the Straits of Florida at the extreme southern end of the continental United States continues to provide an important strategic point from where contingency operations can be conducted if required," [43] echoes the sentiments expressed by Commodore Porter 175 years ago: "It is to the Gulf of Mexico, what Gibraltar is to the Mediterranean."[44]

The USS *Harry S. Truman* visiting Key West on September 29, 2002. The state-of-the-art aircraft carrier stopped in Key West for rest and relaxation on its way to the Persian Gulf to assume its position in the buildup to the war with Iraq. *(U.S. Navy/ Little White House Museum)*

CHAPTER TWO

The Little White House
"I have a White House down in Key West" [1]
–Harry S. Truman, 1947

Although construction on the building that was to become known as the Little White House did not begin until 1890, its genesis dates back to the 1883 letter written by Commander Winn to Captain Johnson. Among other issues addressed in the letter, Commander Winn, the Key West naval station commander from 1877 to 1883 and again from 1885 to 1895, expressed his concern about the lack of housing on the island.

In that letter he described Key West as "the only station where quarters were not provided," resulting in officers having to "rent rooms in the town's boarding houses and those were found to be less than satisfactory." Compounding the problem was the expense of the limited housing that was available: "The expense of living here is at least 50 per cent higher than any other station."[2]

Six years after expressing his concern, and while the station was still under his command, Commander Winn's words were heeded. In the base expansion resulting from the buildup to the Spanish American War, the Navy authorized construction of two "Frame Dwellings" to house the base commandant and the paymaster.[3]

The design specifications by architect George McKay called for two "frame structures, two-stories high, without cellars, and surrounded with piazzas both first and second stories. Main roofs will be double-pitched, and all roofs tinned; sides will be weather-boarded." Both floor plans included a parlor, dining room and kitchen on the first floor and three "chambers" and a bath for each dwelling on the second floor.[4]

The construction of the building, named Officers Quarters A & B, began on January 15, 1890, by New York contractor Rowland Robbins, who had the low bid of $7,489 for this 8,700-square-foot two-family home, a duplex in today's terms.[5]

While the house was built according to federal planning guidelines for military housing, there were architectural considerations made for the tropical climate. The architecture is best characterized as Bahamian or Conch vernacular, reflecting the influence of the New England shipbuilders who had settled in Key West, many via the Bahamas, and translated their skills into the building of houses.

The two-story rectangular mass, the low gabled roof, the horizontal exterior weather-boards, and double-tiered porch with simple wood balustrade are all identifiable architectural features of this building type. Additional features, such as the wood louvered windows, the covered porches, and the elevation off the ground, allowed for optimum air circulation. The Victorian gingerbread decoration was an extension of the influence of the carpenter-builders.[6]

(Above) Photographs of the original building (circa 1890) show it having covered porches on both floors and on all four sides of the house. Later modifications altered this design element, eliminating porches on the back. *(National Archives/Langley Collection)*

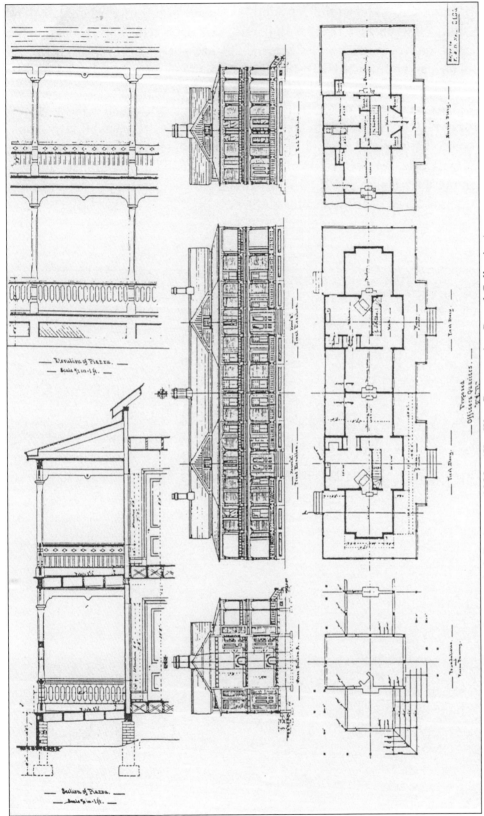

Original floor plan of Officers Quarters A & B, August 1889. (*Key West Preservation Board Collection*)

At the time of the construction of the new officers' quarters, much of Key West obtained its water through rainwater collected in cisterns. The water needs of Quarters A & B were met by two 2,800-gallon cisterns located in the attic. Six brick fireplaces, four downstairs and two upstairs, provided heat in tropical Key West.

While indoor plumbing was not always de rigueur in Key West in the 1890s, this house had such conveniences. A letter written by Commander Winn dated January 25, 1890, requesting changes to the original plans, pointed out that "water closet bowls selected does not require any boxing, simply a seat." Additionally, iron plumbing was brought into the house "upon the recommendation of Plumbers, for the reason that lead pipe was not so healthy for general use." This, he noted, was an important consideration as "there are no plumbers here who can do good lead pipe work."[7] In a letter dated May 3, 1890, Commander Winn again referenced the indoor plumbing, requesting that funds be telegraphed to him to "allow the Plumbing work on washbasins ($54.00) so that there will be no delay in completing the whole structure."[8]

It appears Commander Winn listened to the advice of local builders in making climate-specific changes. The first floor was heightened, "to have a 10 feet stud inside measurement instead of 10 feet 8 inches from floor to floor as per floor plan. this (sic) is recommended by builders here, and all considered that even this was too low for houses in this climate." He requested slat blinds for "front of Houses A and B Officers Quarters (both stories) as they were almost indispensable during the afternoon." The blinds, he suggested, should "be of 7/8 inch stuff 6 inches wide and to be fitted between the pillars or posts on front of Houses. They will add materially to the comfort and the cost will be inside of the appropriation now available." [9]

For safety and comfort reasons, many Key West houses of the time had outdoor cookhouses. Plans for Quarters A & B called for indoor kitchens. However, in a letter written by Paymaster Henry R. Smith, an unsuccessful case was made "that 'cook-house' be allowed as an addition to house 'B', officers quarters." Citing in great detail the weather conditions and the direction of the prevailing winds, he concluded that "house B would be most uncomfortable – situated as it is – wholly covered on the east by the bridle foundry – if cooking were attempted in the range, even in winter."[10]

As the house neared completion, Commander Winn voiced his pleasure in the new quarters in a letter dated May 17, 1890: "I like the location very much and I believe the houses will be very comfortable. They are certainly very pretty and make an excellent appearance."[11] On May 24, 1890, just four months after construction began, Commander Winn reported that the Officers Quarters in Key West were "satisfactorily completed," and the "keys of the houses were handed to me to-day."[12]

Officers Quarters A & B circa 1900. Front view shows its proximity to the water's edge. At this time very little land separated it from the Gulf of Mexico. *(Ill. Postcard Co./Little White House Museum)*

For over 50 years, only a seawall separated Quarters A & B from the Gulf of Mexico, giving it spectacular sunset views. That view, however, was effectively blocked in 1942, when, during the World War II base expansion efforts, the Navy erected a massive gray concrete building on the landfill directly in front of the Little White House. The Naval Administration Building, as it was known, housed the offices of the submarine base land support group. Today it is an upscale condominium complex commanding great views of the harbor.

During the first decade of the twentieth century, at the time Key West was the headquarters of Caribbean communications for the Navy, Quarters A & B were modified into a single family home and renamed "Quarters A – The Commandant's House," for the use of Admiral Lucian Young who served in Key West from 1911 to 1912. A new lawn, tennis courts and gazebo were added, thus securing its position as the base commander's residence.[13]

Quarters A circa 1912. Landscaping, including paths and a gazebo, were added to front of Quarters A for Admiral Lucian Young. Note the tall pole and guy wires of one of the naval communications towers erected in 1906. *(Monroe County Public Library)*

Throughout World War I, Quarters A retained its place as home of the base commandants. However, as a result of the diminishing military presence in Key West at the conclusion of World War I, combined with the effects of the Great Depression, the base was deactivated in 1932, and Officers Quarters A was closed.

The next military buildup of the Key West military base was brought about by World War II and was expansive in scope. Captain C.E. Reordan, USN, became the first commander of both the air station and submarine base, and resided with his family in the reopened Quarters A. After his retirement in 1946, the next base commander, Captain W.J. Suits, moved his quarters to Trumbo Point as he felt that the 8700 square foot quarters was too large.[14]

With this move, Quarters A again stood vacant. A decision was made that would establish its legacy and secure its place in history: Fleet Admiral Chester W. Nimitz, USN, suggested Quarters A on the Naval Station in Key West as a possible vacation spot for President Harry S. Truman.[15]

This suggestion was accepted. Upon President Truman's arrival for his first Key West vacation in November 1946, he wrote his wife, Bess, "I'm in a house built on a Southern plan with galleries all around, upstairs and down. It is the house of the commandant of the submarine base. They have no commandant at present so I'm not ranking anyone out of his house."[16]

The Miami Herald informed the curious public: "The President is occupying the large corner room on the north exposure of the second floor. Just outside his room is a broad veranda, enclosed with jalousies. A few hundred feet away the blue waters of the Gulf of Mexico lap against the sea walls of the submarine base."[17]

As early as the second trip in March 1947, the official presidential daily log made note of the large frame house as being "often referred to as the 'Winter White House.'"[18] Truman himself established the legitimacy of Quarters A as a presidential vacation residence in the opening remarks of his speech at the dedication of the Everglades National Park on December 6, 1947: "I have a White House down in Key West."[19] Following that remark, the name "Little White House" became commonly accepted.

In fact, throughout the course of President Truman's 11 presidential visits, Quarters A became a functioning White House. With each visit, the support and infrastructure necessary for a seamless transition from Washington to the president's Key West vacation spot grew, allowing the affairs of state to continue uninterrupted.

When the president visited the "frame cottage," a description often used by the press, it was filled to capacity. He and his entourage, which included staff and guests, filled every available room, some having to bunk in the same room, some on the extended porches.

The March 1949 official presidential log described the arrangements: "Truman, usual suite, Admiral Foskett and General Vaughan — north center bedroom, Mr. Ross and Mr. Clifford south center bedroom, Mr. Connelly and Mr. Steelman, south bedroom, Mr. Woodward, small bedroom on the second floor, Admiral Leahy and Judge Collet - bedroom on first floor, General Graham 2nd floor porch." The overflow, "members of White House Staff, Press and Secret Service were houses (sic) at Bachelor Officer's Quarters (Building 128) Subsisted at Fleet Sonar School Officer's Mess, located across the street. 106. Also quarters L was used for overflow. *Williamsburg* (the presidential yacht) was also used."[20]

In all that was written during, and later about, President Truman's time at his island retreat, it is well documented that throughout the course of his visits, national and international leaders met with him, correspondence arrived daily in quantity, and legislation was enacted. In a letter written to Mrs. Truman during his fourth visit, the president summed up his schedule: "Have been resting well, but the work comes along just the same. I've been reading and signing messages, executive orders, statements, letters etc. at the usual rate…"[21]

Mrs. Truman did not join her husband in Key West until his fifth visit, on November 7, 1948, one that immediately followed the grueling campaign and subsequent surprise election of Truman over Thomas Dewey. Their daughter, Margaret, who accompanied them, described the personal toll of campaign rigors: "Mother and I joined Dad in Key West for his vacation. We needed the rest almost as much as he did."[22]

The presence of Mrs. Truman in the house, combined with Truman's re-election to a full term, led the Navy to the realization that Key West and the Little White House might be experiencing an increase in presidential visits throughout the next four years. The decision was made to redecorate the Little White House in a style more suitable for the President of the United States.

South side of Little White House in March 1947, prior to renovation. *(U. S. Navy /Harry S. Truman Library)*

Miami-based interior decorator Haygood Lasseter was hired by the Navy to completely redecorate the house for $35,000. In addition to interior design responsibilities, he made structural improvements: some floors were leveled or ramped to eliminate deep steps, and several upstairs bedrooms were enlarged by absorbing the porches on the east side, or back, of the house into the interior floor plan. [23]

In describing his design concept for the presidential retreat, Lasseter explained, "We have tried to plan these quarters in a quality befitting the caliber of guests expected to enjoy their use and in a style designed to be conducive to a maximum of relaxation."[24]

Southwest side of Little White House after the 1949 remodeling, showing expansion of south porch. *(U. S. Navy/Harry S. Truman Library)*

Little White House living room in March 1949, following the Lasseter remodeling. *(U. S. Navy/Harry S. Truman Library)*

Little White House living room in March 1949. Leather inlaid mahogany tables and Hepplewhite styled furnishings brought a new elegance. Colors, popular in the 1940s – avocado, lime, deep blue, gray green, tomato red and bright yellow – were used. *(U.S. Navy/Harry S. Truman Library)*

Ships' models and nautically themed paintings and prints, on loan from the Naval Academy Museum, decorated the house.[25] Comfortable reading chairs with good lighting filled the spaces of this pre-television home. The radio-phonograph in the living room was a popular diversion. The president and staff enjoying listening to prize fights, sporting events, and music, which included Truman's favorite, Chopin. It was here, in March 1947, that President Truman heard his daughter's first public singing broadcast with the Detroit Symphony.[26]

Truman was an accomplished pianist who enjoyed playing the piano kept on board the presidential yacht, the USS *Williamsburg*, which accompanied him to the island retreat. When the president was in residence in Key West, the piano was moved from the *Williamsburg* to the living room in the Little White House for his use.[27] Today, the piano is on display in the living room of the Little White House Museum.

The redecorated dining room in 1949. It looks now as it did then and is currently used, as it was during President Truman's visits, to host visiting guests and dignitaries. "As the dining room will accommodate a maximum of 14, the party schedule was so arranged that no more than 14 guests would be present at any one time."[28] Secretary of State Colin Powell hosted a luncheon in the dining room in April 2000 for the presidents of Armenia and Azerbaijan during peace talks between these two countries held at the Little White House. On the buffet are roosters that were at one time symbols of the Democratic party. *(U.S. Navy/ Harry S. Truman Library)*

The south porch, used by Truman as a recreation room, was enlarged in the remodeling to accommodate the increasing number of staffers coming to Key West. It was here he was presented with his prized solid mahogany poker table built by the cabinet shop staff of the base.

Local civil service employees Charles Robinson, Jack Steadman and Hastings Adams duplicated the poker table that was on board the USS *Williamsburg* for the president's use in the Little White House. The round top and hexagonal base were made of South African mahogany. The details included built-in chip holders, glass holders, and ashtrays made of 50-mm recycled shell cases. While others watched first-run motion pictures in the living room, Truman and a quorum usually enjoyed a lively game of poker on the south porch at the specially-made table.[29]

The corner of the expanded and remodeled south porch in March 1949, with the poker table in place. In this photograph, the poker table is covered by a tabletop constructed of mahogany marquetry, cleverly concealing the table's poker facilities, thereby allowing it to also serve as an informal dining space. *(U. S. Navy/Harry S. Truman Library)*

The remodeling of the house took less than four months to complete and was finished before the president arrived on his sixth visit. On March 6, 1949, he wrote his wife expressing his delight with the change, "The place is all redecorated. The porches have been leveled up so there are no steps from the dining room – new furniture and everything. I've a notion to move the Capital to Key West and just stay."[30]

His description of Mrs. Truman's bedroom was effusive: "They have fixed you up a palatial bedroom next to mine. You've never seen a nicer one."[31]

Mrs. Truman's bedroom in March 1949. *(U. S. Navy/Harry S. Truman Library)*

The president apparently found the renovated house so comfortable that on the morning after his March 6, 1949 arrival, he slept until 9:30 am – very unusual for a man who, while in Washington, usually arose at 5:30 am. "Nobody had ever heard of the President's sleeping so much of the morning away and Mr. Hassett, of the President's secretariat said he could not explain it unless it was the soothing deep blue tone of his newly-renovated bedroom in the winter White House."[32]

President Truman's bedroom, following the 1949 remodeling. *(U. S. Navy/Harry S. Truman Library)*

President Truman returned to the Little White House five more times after the renovation. Following his eleventh and final visit as president in March 1952, the Navy reclaimed it for officers' housing. No longer a presidential site, the Little White House was converted into a duplex and reverted to its original name, Quarters A & B. One side was occupied by Rear Admiral George Tower; the other side by Lieutenant Commander Sid Chapman.[33]

Although the Little White House had been redecorated specifically to accommodate the president, the house and furnishings were considered to be Navy property and were kept for use by the Navy. The presidential furniture was redistributed between the two sides of the duplex. The fact that it was used by the President of the United States gave it no appreciable value; it was merely Navy issue furniture to be put to good use.

The photographs on the following page illustrate just how the original furniture was refinished, reupholstered and reused alongside personal furniture belonging to the officers who resided in the Little White House during the post-presidential years.

(Above) The dining room in the Little White House set for dinner during one of President Truman's visits following the 1949 remodeling. Note the light finish of the wood and the floral upholstery on the chairs. *(U. S. Navy/Harry S. Truman Library)* (Below) Dining room in Officers Quarters A during the post-presidential era. Chairs are stripped, cherry stained and covered with damask upholstery. Gone is the buffet used during the Truman era, the residents preferring their own. *(Wright Langley /Little White House)*

In 1957 Rear Admiral Frances McCorkle took command of the Key West Naval Station and established Quarters A as his command headquarters, converting it back to a single-family home. He carefully had the building and furnishings restored to their 1949 appearance, thereby creating a Truman-era ambiance.[34] Although his intent in doing so is not known, were it not for his decision to preserve the look of the presidential Little White House, much of the furniture might have been permanently moved to other locations, forever lost to history.

Between 1957 and 1974, the Little White House continued to be used as the residence of various base commandants. Although Truman never again stayed in the Little White House, the base commanders hosted the former president when he came to call during his visits to Key West as a private citizen. The residence was also made available to President Eisenhower and President Kennedy for meetings each held in Key West.

Following Truman's death on December 26, 1972, the Navy public works department drew up plans for a proposed President Truman Museum. Among other proposed changes, the front lawn was to be altered with the addition of a reflecting pool and fountains.[35] However, the Navy was experiencing considerable downsizing at the time and, before these plans could be executed, the Key West Naval Station was de-established. For the next twelve years, between 1974 and 1986, the Little White House and surrounding buildings were abandoned.

A boarded up Little White House in January 1976, waiting for its future to be determined. *(Florida Department of Commerce/Florida Photo Collection/Department of State)*

The citizens of Key West continued to hope that President Truman's Little White House might someday become museum and worked towards that objective. In 1974, while the house was still boarded up, a first crucial step was taken to recognize its historic significance: it was listed in the National Register of Historic Places.

Military downsizing in October 1977 led to the Navy's decision to turn over the Little White House, along with sixty-nine other closed Navy buildings in Key West, to local control. The responsibility for these properties was a shared arrangement between the civilian Key West Redevelopment Agency and the City of Key West.

As part of the transfer arrangement, the artifacts and original furnishings used by Truman were inventoried and given to the City of Key West to store and safeguard. Guarded by one watchman, the house and its remaining contents suffered from neglect, minor vandalism and petty theft.

The Little White House living room during the period of its abandonment between 1974 through 1986. Fireplace appears to have been used by vagrants. *(Little White House Museum)*

View of living room looking towards the foyer during the same period of abandonment. *(Little White House Museum)*

Correspondence between the Key West Redevelopment Agency and the City of Key West from 1977 through 1983 points to the constant concern and frustration over continued break-ins and vandalism at the Little White House. In one letter, dated July 27, 1979, the City Coordinator for Federal Properties complained that "items were missing from the south porch." Indeed, a careful inventory showed "items listed on an attached sheet appear to be missing." Furthermore, a search of the attic discovered "a large, partially burned torch made of rags wired to a broom handle or other large stick, which the intruders must have needed to see their way through the pitch-blackness." There was more than monetary value at stake; most of the items were "irreplaceable and of intrinsic historic value rather than of extrinsic value."[36]

A major preservation plan for this important historic site was proposed in 1979 by Key West Mayor Charles (Sonny) McCoy and Florida Senator Richard Stone as part of a larger redevelopment plan for the entire base. The aggressive master plan was an effort to boost the local economy of Key West, suffering in the wake of the Navy's departure. The presidential site was to be a second presidential retreat, complementing Camp David, now the retreat of choice. The surrounding area was to include new homes, a large marina and hotel, retail and office space, and a cruise port.[37]

The plan for the presidential retreat called for the destruction of the Naval Administration Building, thereby reinstating the original water view from the Little White House, and the addition of a swimming pool, tennis courts and putting green. An interpretive center for tourists, to be used when the president was not in residence, was proposed for the red brick machine shop located on one side of the Little White House. Building 21, located on the other side, would serve as headquarters for the Secret Service and presidential staff.[38]

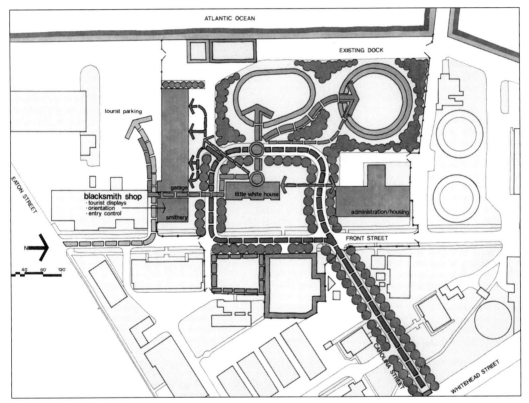

Architectural rendering for a proposal for the development of the Little White House, Key West, Florida (1979). Concept by Senator Richard "Dick" Stone and Mayor Charles McCoy. Prepared by Greenleaf/Telesca, Planners, Engineers, Architects, 1451 Brickell Avenue, Miami, Florida. (*Little White House Museum*)

Despite this and other local efforts, no agreement could be reached for the development of this important property. The U.S. government was undertaking cost cutting measures in the late 1970s, and had no interest in funding a second presidential retreat.

Finally, the General Services Administration declared the base and the buildings surplus land, selling them at a public auction on September 10, 1986. The historic integrity of nineteen historic properties on the base, comprised of the Little White House (Quarters A); the Custom House (Building 91); the Coast Guard Building (Building #1), known today as Clinton Square Market; Quarters L (where President Eisenhower once resided); and the Marine Hospital, dating from 1846, was protected by a Memorandum of Agreement for renovation and rehabilitation of historic sites drawn up on March 13, 1986, between the Department of Interior and any potential purchaser.[39]

With a high bid of $17.4 million for the large parcel, Pritam Singh, an American developer from Maine, took control of the property. The Little White House was recognized as the most important historic building in the complex of buildings included in the sale, and was protected under the Memorandum of Agreement.

The state of Florida was also interested in ensuring the historic preservation of Florida's only presidential site. On January 1, 1987, through a complex arrangement with the state, Pritam Singh exchanged the Little White House building and surrounding grounds for some submerged lands off of Key West.

The state of Florida now had control of the historic Little White House and set about planning its restoration. Nature had taken its toll on the boarded-up building. It is said that in the tropics it does not take long for an abandoned area to return to its natural state; that this phenomenon had occurred was evident. The amount of damage the house had incurred during the twelve years of neglect was significant, and the state government did not have the estimated $1 million needed to restore it.

Mr. Singh offered to restore the Little White House as a concessionaire, operating it as a museum for the state of Florida. The state agreed, entering into a long-term lease with protective provisions. Mr. Singh hired well-known Miami historian Arva Moore Parks to oversee the restoration, and Elizabeth Erhbar of Tallahassee as preservationist.

Their task was daunting. The project involved thousands of details, research, and years of work, as it had to comply with the terms spelled out in the Memorandum of Agreement: "The Little White House...will be fully restored to accurately recover the form and details of their historic appearance. Restoration of the Little White House will return the building to its 'Truman era' appearance."[40]

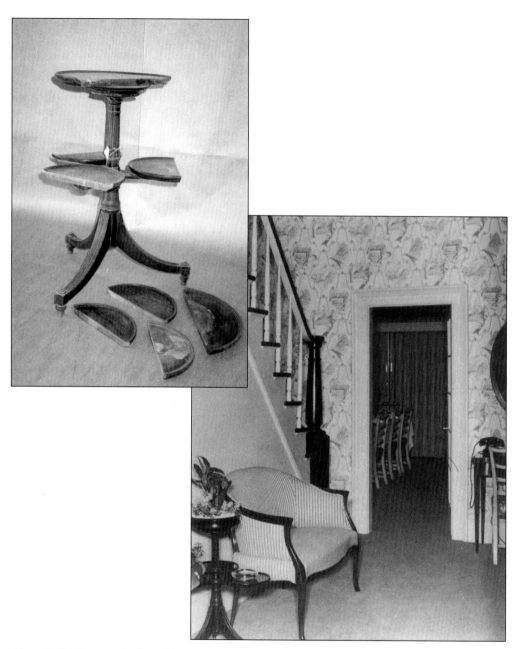

(Above left) Foyer table, found broken in the abandoned Little White House. (Above right) The same table, carefully restored and in its original place in the foyer. *(Little White House Museum)*

Before the project could be completed, there was a downturn in the real estate market. In 1990, Mr. and Mrs. Henry Drettman of Detroit, Michigan, purchased Mr. Singh's interests in the property and completed the restoration under a management contract with the state.

The piano (above left) and the poker table (above right) had been stored at the East Martello Museum during the time the Little White House was abandoned. Perceived as symbols of the personal side of Truman, their return to their rightful place in the Little White House was an important milestone in the remodeling effort. *(Little White House Museum)*

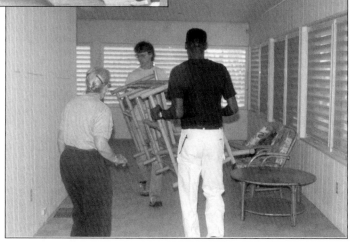

March 1991: Moving in at last! (Left) Elizabeth Erhbar expressing her excitement. (Right) The furniture, found and carefully restored, is moved back in. (*Little White House Museum*)

The house was now finally complete. After nearly four years and close to $1 million dollars, the Harry S. Truman Little White House Museum, restored to its Truman era-appearance, was ready for its grand opening in April 1991.

Elizabeth Newland, a landscape architect involved in the restoration from the start, was named the museum's first executive director. She was followed in this position by Hal Walsh, a retired stockbroker and historian.

Four major exhibits were created during Mr. Walsh's directorship: an exhibit on President Truman's "Key West uniforms;" a commemoration of the 40th anniversary of President Eisenhower's visit; a commemoration of the 35th anniversary of the 1961 summit between Prime Minister Macmillan and President Kennedy; and a special Spanish American War exhibit entitled, "William McKinley – Our Forgotten Commander-in-Chief."

Yet another change in the management of the Little White House Museum occurred in 1999. The Drettman family sold their management company to Historic Tours of America, Inc., a Key West-based national tour, attraction and retail company, headed by Ed Swift and Chris Belland. Robert Wolz, historian and former general manager of Historic Tours of America's Old Town Trolley, was named executive director.

Baby boomers themselves, Mr. Swift, Mr. Belland, and Mr. Wolz were concerned that younger visitors to the Little White House Museum might not fully comprehend the impact nor appreciate the accomplishments of the Truman presidency.

To ensure the full respect and stature of this important presidential site, they immediately invested over $200,000 in the building and in two new permanent exhibits. Under the guidance of Robert Wolz, *The President Truman Gallery* is now filled with photographs, film clips and artifacts relating to President Truman; *Key West – Where Presidents Vacation* features an array of photographs from 1880 to the present of American presidents and other world leaders who have visited not only the Little White House, but who have visited and vacationed in Key West and the Florida Keys as well.

Daily, year-round tours of the home capture time frozen. Guests to the museum visit all the rooms used by President Truman. The furnishings and décor, combined with the stories told by knowledgeable tour guides, transport guests back in time. Historic Tours of America, Inc., and the not-for-profit Key West - Harry S. Truman Foundation, Inc., continue to expand the Little White House Museum's collection of presidential artifacts to further its mission of education, restoration and preservation.

Little White House Museum tours provide the opportunity to bring to life an important time in the Truman presidency. *(Little White House Museum)*

Little White House Museum and grounds in 2002. *(Photo by Garren Zuck)*

CHAPTER THREE

The Presidential Visits

"The business of government never stops no matter where the President goes – it follows him."[1]
–Harry S. Truman, 1951

Following Harry S. Truman's assumption of the presidency in the wake of President Roosevelt's death, finding a suitable retreat for him proved to be a challenge. A planned brief summer cruise aboard the USS *Williamsburg* off the coast of Maine was cancelled because, as expressed by the president in an August 22, 1946, letter to his wife, "The Maine coast cruise ended in a blow up. Everybody and his brother whom I didn't want to see tried by every hook or crook to rope me into letting him come aboard or having me be seen with him. So I just cancelled the trip."[2]

In early September 1946, the president tried a brief cruise to Bermuda. It was not a pleasant trip. He recounted the experience in a letter to Mrs. Truman: "It was sunny and the sea was calm. But by dinnertime we'd run into rain squalls and a rough sea…. I became seasick at the dinner table and rushed to my quarters and to bed. Stayed there most of yesterday."[3]

By early autumn, the president had developed a persistent cough, and rest in a warm climate was prescribed by his personal physician. What was needed in addition to a warm location, however, was a place remote enough so as to discourage visitation, but still protected and within easy communication of Washington, D.C. Fleet Admiral Chester W. Nimitz's suggestion of the vacant Officers Quarters A on the Naval Station in Key West fit all those parameters.

The appeal of this island getaway was explained by Bradford Mobley, the *Miami Herald's* Washington correspondent, "President Truman came to the southernmost part of the United States because it is easy to get to, and provides him a degree of seclusion when he arrives." Furthermore, "nobody bothers Truman in Key West. He is given a hearty reception on arrival and then is left alone." This president liked to "collect those friends or officials he wants to take along," and going to "a spot where he knows no one appeals to him."[4]

It began as one-time vacation getaway. The decision to return again and again, however, quickly transformed Quarters A and the 2-mile by 4-mile island into the presidential retreat of choice. President Truman chose to vacation in Key West, residing in Quarters A, eleven times for a total of 175 days, beginning on November 16, 1946, and continuing through March 27, 1952. In total, the 33rd President of the United States spent approximately 10% of his time in office in Key West.

The presidential entourage started out small, but with each visit the support staff grew. Commander Rigdon, USN, President Truman's assistant Naval aide, chronicled the staff increase in his book, *The White House Sailor*: "On our first visit, in 1946, the President's needs were provided by sixteen persons, including cooks,

Reprinted with permission, Cooke Communications.

stewards, clerical and communications personnel, but not including the ever-present force of Secret Service agents. On the eleventh and final outing there, in 1952, a second house in addition to the Little White House and the Presidential yacht was needed to accommodate the fifty-seven staffers and service assistants."[5]

Much of the information available on the details of Truman's eleven visits comes from the official daily presidential logs kept by Commander Rigdon. These logs provide a meticulous account of all the daily activities, offering a rare and personal glimpse into the working vacation routine.

These official logs, along with presidential correspondence, letters, books, photographs, and the historic perspective gained by the passage of time, collectively provide evidence of the far-reaching decisions addressed during the years Truman resided in the Little White House. That decisions of great importance were made while he was visiting the Little White House is speculative; that they were discussed and pondered there is not.

This notion is supported in an article in the *Miami Herald* dated December 7, 1947: "A year ago he flew down after making a major decision at the White House to conduct his cold war with John L. Lewis (United Mineworkers union president). Last March he took off in the "Sacred Cow" (the presidential plane) for the Boca Chica air base after delivering his "Truman doctrine" message to Congress. This time he came to prepare himself for the next step in his foreign policy. It will be outlined in his forthcoming message to congress on the Marshall Plan."

Testing the Waters

*"This place is what I hoped it would be
and what I was certain it would not be."*[6]
–Harry S. Truman, 1946

The president first arrived in Key West on November 17, 1946, and followed doctor's orders. "I have arranged a schedule so that I get up at 7:30 (two hours later than I usually do), go over and have a swim, have breakfast at nine and then go to a nice sand beach a half mile away and get sun and sea water. Come back at noon, have lunch at one and then a nap and sit around and talk until dinner at seven, go to bed when I get ready and then do it over. I've just returned from the beach after trying out the schedule and my cough and cold are nearly gone already."[7]

The Truman side stroke. *(U. S. Navy/Harry S. Truman Library)*

The president's catch of the day included a six-pound grouper and a three-pound yellowtail.[8]
(U. S. Navy/Harry S. Truman Library)

The visit, however, was more than just rest and relaxation. As protocol would dictate, time was scheduled for the president to inspect the submarine base and the air station.

On November 21, 1946, President Truman and his party of twenty-two boarded the captured German submarine U2513 and set sail. Members of the press were not invited to attend because of the many secret experimental devises on board.[9] This first submarine dive by an American president achieved a depth of 450 feet, but "at no time was the slightest apprehension felt by any member of our party for his safety.[10]

President Truman leaving the German submarine U2513 in December 1947, after having received a certificate from Rear Admiral James Fife, commander of the Atlantic Fleet submarine force, commemorating his milestone dive on the submarine on November 21, 1946.[11] *(U.S. Navy/Harry S. Truman Library)*

President Truman inspecting gun sights at Boca Chica Naval Air Station. *(Little White House Museum)*

(Above) The president and his party arriving at the Fort Jefferson National Monument, 70 miles west of Key West, after having made the trip aboard the destroyer, *Stribling*. (Below) Mr. Russell Gibbs, fort custodian, gave the presidential party a tour of the Civil War era fort. They visited the cell where Dr. Samuel Mudd, the physician who set the leg of John Wilkes Booth following Abraham Lincoln's assassination, was held prisoner.[12]   (*U.S. Navy/Truman Library Collection; Little White House Museum*)

As his first visit to Key West came to end, the *Key West Citizen* quoted the president as saying, "I love it here!"   When asked by City Commissioner Louis Carbonell if he would return, he replied, "You bet I will."[13]

SECOND VISIT: MARCH 12-19, 1947

Isolationism Ends: The Truman Doctrine

"It must be the policy of the United States to support free peoples who are resisting attempted subjugation by armed minorities or by outside pressures."[14]
–Harry S. Truman, 1947

The president had planned a Caribbean vacation to begin March 8, 1947, that was to include a brief stay in Key West and a 15-day sail on the USS *Williamsburg*. These plans were scrapped on March 7th, when "the White House announced that the president's Caribbean vacation had been postponed because of developments."[15]

The following day there was a clarification of the cancellation: "Truman sat in the White House, rather than in Key West, weighing the most momentous decision since war's end — whether to reshape historic American foreign policy by calling for the direct intervention in the internal affairs of Greece."[16] Communist-backed rebels had been threatening civil war in both Greece and Turkey. Britain was disengaging its influence from the region by withdrawing 40,000 troops and ending its foreign aid to these nations, thereby threatening a collapse of the governments in Greece, Turkey and Iran.

President Truman addressed Congress in early March 1947, asking for 400 million dollars in military and economic aid to Greece and Turkey. Marking the beginning of a new foreign policy direction for the United States, President Truman stated the reasoning behind the foundation of his request eloquently: "This is no more a frank recognition that totalitarian regimes imposed on free peoples, by direct or indirect aggression, undermine the foundations of international peace and hence the security of the United States."[17]

With this relief effort, which became known as the Truman Doctrine, a major foreign policy precedent was established.

Following the address to Congress, the president's physician, Brigadier General Graham, told the United Press International he had once again given President Truman "positive instructions for absolute rest."[18]

On March 12, 1947, the day after receiving those instructions, the president left for Key West. To his daughter, Margaret, he wrote, "We had a pleasant flight from Washington. Your old Dad slept for 750 or 800 miles – three hours, and we were traveling from 250 to 300 miles an hour. No one, not even me (your mother would say) knew how very tired and worn to a frazzle the Chief Executive had become. This terrible decision I had to make has been over my head for about six weeks."[19]

Columnist Earl Adams put it this way in the *Miami Herald*: "The job of the United States President is an exacting and tiresome one even in tranquil times. The constant strain saps up the energy of the nation's chief executive. Mr. Truman is no exception, but one thing is a certainty, he is determined to get away from Washington and back down here (to Key West) whenever he finds himself in need of rest."[20] Arriving for his second visit, the president reminded Key West Mayor William Demerett, "I told you I would be back. This is my favorite vacation spot."[21]

Issues surrounding the Balkan crisis underscored his visit. The president was in constant contact with Washington concerning the Truman Doctrine and received reports from Secretary of State George Marshall on Russian reaction to the Truman Doctrine.[22]

RUSSIA LOOKS AT THE TRUMAN DOCTRINE

Efimov, Moscow Literary Gazette

The Russian criticized the Truman Doctrine. Here, Marshall is caricatured berating a Greek monarchist, who, clad in a bottomless barrel through which American aid had poured, pleads for more funds to fight against the Russian-backed guerrillas. *(Reprinted with permission of the Miami Herald Publishing Company)*

The Russian newspaper, *Izvestia*, was also critical of the president's request for aid to Greece and Turkey, considering it a "fresh intrusion," threatening the independence of those two nations and short-circuiting the United Nations.[23]

Truman's reaction to the Russian criticism was described by the *Key West Citizen*: "President Truman today turned a stony silence on editorials in the semi-official Soviet newspaper, *Izvestia*, criticizing his address on aid to Greece, and headed out into the Gulf Stream for a day of fishing."[24]

Margaret Sings; a Friendship Begins

The president almost cut his vacation short to fly to Detroit for personal reasons. His daughter, Margaret, was to have her debut as a professional soloist with the Detroit Symphony on March 16, 1947, and he understandably did not want to miss this once-in-a-lifetime occasion.

The dilemma was solved by local businessman John Spottswood, owner of the only radio station in town, WKWF, who, eager to have the president stay in Key West, offered to have him hear his daughter via radio in the comfort of the Little White House living room.

There was one major problem to this arrangement: Spottswood's station was affiliated with the Mutual Broadcasting Network, and Miss Truman was singing on the American Broadcasting Network. Mr. Spottswood did everything possible to arrange the network change for one hour, but could not obtain FCC approval in time. When he reluctantly informed Truman of the FCC holdup, the president picked up the phone, and very quickly the "road was unblocked." The stage was now set for the performance to be heard in Key West.[25]

John Spottswood, the owner of the only radio station in Key West at the time of Truman's 1947 visit. *(Harry S. Truman Little White House)*

Nonetheless, so concerned was John Spottswood with the temporary nature of the technical aspects of the broadcast arrangement that, when he arrived to be with the president during the broadcast, he told the driver of his car, "Let it run. I might be leaving in a hurry!"[26]

Throughout the performance, which went off without a hitch, the nervous 26-year-old Spottswood, who sat with the president, "did not hear one note."[27] At the conclusion of the event, when asked by Truman if he enjoyed the performance, the young station manager replied, "Not a damn Mr. President," quickly explaining his anxiety about the possibility of technical problems that could have arisen during the broadcast but, to his relief, did not.[28]

This act of kindness would not be forgotten. With it began a friendship that lasted for the remainder of Truman's life.

Margaret Truman receiving flowers following her performance with the Detroit Symphony on March 16, 1947. *(U.S. Navy/Harry S. Truman Library)*

THIRD VISIT: DECEMBER 3-8, 1947

The Everglades National Park Dedication

"Our parks are but one part of the national effort to conserve our natural resources. Upon these resources our life as a nation depends."[29]

–Harry S. Truman, 1947

President Truman's third visit in December 1947 followed a now-standard routine. He was seen off from Washington by Mrs. Truman for a three-and-a-half hour flight. He landed at Boca Chica Naval Air Station, where military and local officials welcomed him. Finally, his motorcade traveled down the Overseas Highway and into Key West, passing by citizens of the island community who lined the streets along the way to welcome him. Upon his arrival at the Little White House, the presidential flag was raised above the Administration Building across the street, a signal to all that the president was in residence.

Enlisted men in dress white uniforms "manned the rails" along the route to the Little White House to honor the visiting president. *(Photo courtesy Percy Curry)*

Once settled in his quarters at the Little White House, President Truman and his party relaxed as much as possible, fishing and swimming. Nonetheless, calls with his Washington staff occupied much of his time.

On this trip, concerns with the rebuilding of Europe were mounting: "Press Secretary Charles Ross said Mr. Truman had been thinking about the Marshall Plan during his stay here… No definite date has been set for presentation of the plan to Congress. He expressed his belief it would soon be after the President returns to Washington."[30]

On December 6, 1947, the president took a daylong trip to Naples and Everglades City, Florida, where he dedicated the Everglades National Park. In his dedication speech, Truman spoke of the unique new national park as a "project whose great value lies in the enrichment of the human spirit." He took the occasion to express his concerns for the value of the conservation of the nation's resources. He encouraged the diligent use and management of natural resources, while cautioning, "We have to remain constantly vigilant to prevent raids by those who would selfishly exploit our common heritage for their private gain." He showed enormous foresight by clearly recognizing the long-term importance of Florida's Everglades as a "land, tranquil in its quiet beauty, serving not as the source of water but as the last receiver of it."[31]

Over 5000 guests, including 150 Seminole Indians, attended the dedication of Everglades National Park. At the time it was the third largest national park, exceeded only by Yellowstone and Mt. McKinley.[32] *(U.S. Navy/Harry S. Truman Library)*

President Truman delivering his address from the palm-decorated dais at the dedication of the Everglades National Park. *(U.S. Navy/Harry S. Truman Library)*

After the dedication, the president himself drove his party back to Naples to board the plane for their return to the Little White House in Key West.[33]

FOURTH VISIT: FEBRUARY 20 – MARCH 5, 1948

The Palestine Problem
"United States policy will not be unilateral."[34]
–U. S. Ambassador Warren R. Austin, 1948

President Truman's fourth visit, in late February and early March 1948, was a busy one. He combined his Key West vacation with a goodwill mission to Puerto Rico, the Virgin Islands, and Guantanamo, Cuba. While on this trip, the "complex problem in Palestine"[35] demanded his attention.

While en route from Guantanamo to Key West on the USS *Williamsburg*, the president received and reviewed the text of a U.S. policy address on the issue of Palestine that was to be delivered the following day to the United Nations Security Council by U. S. Ambassador Warren R. Austin.

Immediately following Ambassador Austin's speech, the press received the president's statement from the *Williamsburg*: "The Palestine problem has been, and is, the deep concern of this government. It has been given the most careful consideration by me, the Cabinet, and other responsible government officials. The U.S. position has been developed through long and exhaustive study and many consultations. This position has been accurately presented by Ambassador Austin in his speech before the Security Council today."[36]

In brief, the United States position was supportive of the recommendations adopted by the General Assembly on November 29, 1947, to put in place "procedures which we considered most adapted to obtaining a broad and impartial expression of world opinion on the problem which would result in a just and workable solution commending itself to the mandatory power and to the people of Palestine."[37]

Ambassador Austin stated that "United States policy will not be unilateral," rather United States would, "take such action as the Security Council may deem proper with respect to either the Jewish or Arab State if by April 1, 1948, a provisional council of government cannot be selected for that State, or, if selected, cannot carry out its functions." However, Ambassador Austin expressed the concerns of the United States about the potential "threat or use of force, or by incitement to force, on the part of the states or people outside Palestine."[38]

The U.S., however, would consider supporting a possible decision by the Security Council "to use armed force to maintain international peace in connection with Palestine," in order to "prevent aggression against Palestine from the outside," but not if the objective was "enforcing partition."[39]

With this important policy decision behind him, the president arrived in Key West on February 20, 1948, where the "weather was perfect for a vacation and full opportunity was taken for rest and relaxation."[40] Despite the change of venue, his work, and the world's need for his diplomacy, went on.

The logs of this visit reflect an increase in the level of activity between Washington and the Little White House. Early each morning, Truman met with staff and advisors. Each was given his assignment, reporting to the president later in the day. Telephone communication with Cabinet members occurred almost daily. Mail arrived, and bills were routinely signed.

The White House mail was delivered to the president...having been flown down from Washington via Navy plane.[41]   (*U.S. Navy/Harry S. Truman Library*)

President Truman working at his desk in the Little White House living room. In the White House mail pouches on this visit were numerous pieces of legislation, including S316, S402, S500, S551, HR1350, HR3726, HR4141, and HR5525 which were received and signed by the president.[42] *(U. S. Navy/Harry S. Truman Library)*

The press was ever present. Press conferences, such as this one, were usually held on the lawn of the Little White House each Thursday, with daily news briefings by Press Secretary Charlie Ross, who fended off hot topics with "No comment." or "I don't know."[43] *(U. S. Navy/Harry S. Truman Library)*

"At a special ceremony held in the living room of (the Little White House on February 28, 1948) the President signed HR–4127, 'An Amendment to the Civil Service Retirement Act.' The President used fifteen pens in signing the bill, which were later distributed to the various sponsors of the bill and those who were helpful in seeing that it was enacted."[44]

On February 29, 1948, President Truman addressed the nation live from the Little White House via the facilities of the Spottswood-owned WKWF of the American Broadcasting Company, seeking support for the American Red Cross.

His impassioned speech reminded the American people that the "errands of mercy (of the Red Cross) represent a shining chapter in the annals of relief-giving." At the conclusion of the radio address, Truman acknowledged his awareness of the dissension his policies were creating throughout the country: "In this great cause it matters not how we may differ on the pressing issues of the day. Beneath the flag of the Red Cross we are a united people."[45]

Despite the busy pace, the president summed up his reaction to being in Key West instead of Washington in a letter written to Mrs. Truman the day before his departure, "The weather here is ideal. It is hell to have to go back to slavery and the bickerings that I'll have to face from now on, but it must be done."[46]

Many in the presidential party apparently shared those sentiments: "All passengers reported a smooth trip up from Key West, but were jolted by the sub-freezing weather that greeted them as they disembarked at Washington".[47]

FIFTH VISIT: NOVEMBER 7-21, 1948

Bess Arrives

"We needed a rest almost as much as he did."[48]

–Margaret Truman

The November 1948 trip was a victory celebration. Truman arrived at the Little White House ready to recover from the hard-fought political campaign that led to his surprise upset over Tom Dewey. The president had traveled over 31,000 miles that summer, campaigning via his famous whistle stop train tour, after which he wrote his sister, Mary, "I didn't know I was so tired until I sat down."[49]

On the president's past visits, his entourage of staff and guests was made up of men only. As his daughter, Margaret, explained, "Mother saw it as an all-male setup and thought Dad would have a better time horsing around with Charlie Ross (his press secretary) and Admiral Leahy (his Navy aide), playing poker, and drinking a little bourbon beyond the range of her critical eye."[50] This time, however, Mrs. Truman and Margaret joined him in Key West.

The First Family on the Little White House lawn in November 1948, enjoying the warm Key West weather. *(U.S. Navy/Harry S. Truman Library)*

Margaret enjoyed beach activities like volleyball. The daily logs also reveal that she was escorted to a number of evening dances by single members of the officer corps.[51] *(U. S. Navy/Truman Library Collection)*

Mrs. Truman spent time reading murder mysteries and fishing.[52] She loved to fish and tried her luck at deep-sea fishing on several occasions during this vacation. Of his fishing, however, the president once said, "I am not a fisherman. When I take the madam fishing, she likes to fish, I put the bait on the hook, go and sit down and read and when the fish comes in I go and take it off the hook."[53] *(U.S. Navy/Harry S. Truman Library)*

Visitors came and went. Here, President Truman welcomes Vice President-elect Alben Barkley and Leslie Biffle, secretary of the Democratic Policy Committee, to the Little White House on November 9, 1948. *(U.S. Navy/Harry S. Truman Library)*

The president and Sam Rayburn, future Speaker of the House, who joined him during the November 1948 visit, are pictured at the Navy dock with the USS *Williamsburg* in the background. *(U.S. Navy/Harry S. Truman Library)*

In November 1948, the president's staff and advisors arrived to work on the administration's current program. Front row (l to r) William Hassett, vice president-elect; Senator Barkley, President Truman; Admiral William Leahy, USN; John Steelman. Back row (l to r) Donald Dawson; Eben Ayers; Col. Robert Landry, USA; General Harry Vaughn, USA; Leslie Biffle; Clark Clifford; Stanley Woodward; Brig. General Wallace Graham, USA; Capt. Robert Dennison, USN; William Bray; Jonathan Daniels. *(U.S. Navy/Harry S. Truman Library)*

The presidential log documented yet another series of guests: "At 12:30 p.m., the Honorable James V. Forrestal, Secretary of Defense, called on the President. Secretary Forrestal had come down from Washington in a naval aircraft (R-5-D). He was accompanied to Key West by Major General A.M. Gruenther, USA, Mr. Harold Hinton, Mr. Max Leva, and Colonel Robert J. Wood, USA."[54] The press, however, speculated that Secretary of Defense Forrestal was in Key West to talk with the president, "probably about critical Asiatic and European affairs and his own retirement from the cabinet."[55]

International issues continued to be of concern. As reported by the press, "The Little White House at Key West confirmed that the President has received a letter directly from Chiang Kai-shek, president of the Chinese government, asking for direct United States military and economic aid against the Chinese Communists."[56]

(Left) Defense Secretary James V. Forrestal with President Truman on the lawn of the Little White House on November 18, 1948. *(U. S. Navy/Little White House Museum)*

(Below) The president and his luncheon guests at the Little White House on November 18, 1948. Front row (l to r) Defense Secretary Forrestal; President Truman; Florida Senator Claude Pepper. Rear row (l to r) Mr. Fitzpatrick, New York Democratic state chairman; Mr. Warren, governor-elect of Florida; the Honorable George Smathers, member of Congress (Fourth District of Florida, which included Key West); Mr. Griffin, a prominent central Florida citrus grower; and Mr. Leonard Hicks, of Chicago, Illinois, and operator of the Casa Marina Hotel in Key West.[57] *(U. S. Navy/Little White House Museum)*

The official mail brought from Washington contained an item requiring the president's signature: an executive order prescribing a new coat of arms, seal, and flag for the Vice President of the United States.[58]

The changes to the vice president's seal mirrored the changes made to the presidential seal four years earlier by President Truman with his signing of Executive Order 9648 on October 24, 1945.

The changes to the presidential seal included turning the head of the American eagle to face the talon holding the olive branch rather than facing the arrows. This change reflected Truman's belief that America was a nation seeking peace, not war. The inclusion of a circle of stars, representing all the states, symbolized the president as the leader of all the people in the Union.[59]

With the prospect of having Truman visiting Key West for the next four years, and with the possibility of having the first family accompany him more often, the Navy concluded it was time to remodel Quarters A. The renovation, which included enlarging some of the rooms and redecorating all of them in a traditional décor with a tropical flair, was accomplished in time for the president's next visit four months later.

The War of the Oranges

"Hurt Floridans are suspecting a fifth columnist from California."[60]

The remodeling made the Little White House much more accommodating for the president and the increasing number of staffers and guests coming to Key West.

The opportunity to hold informal meetings gave Truman a chance to discuss pressing issues with high-ranking officials in a relaxed atmosphere. The chief justice of the United States, Frederick M. Vinson, vacationed with the president on this trip, residing in the Little White House. Truman even asked the chief justice to consider running for president in the 1952 election.[61]

The presidential party in the Little White House living room on March 16, 1949. Chief Justice Frederick M. Vinson is seated on the sofa to the left of the president. *(U.S. Navy/Harry S. Truman Library)*

(Above) President Truman greeting General George Marshall and Mr. Pawley, former ambassador to Brazil, at the entrance of the Little White House. They flew in for meetings and lunch on March 15, 1949.[62] *(U.S. Navy/Harry S. Truman Library)*

(Below) The increasingly large quantity of arriving mail continued to receive press coverage: "Chief Ship's Clerk Prophet arrived at the Little White House at 2:30 p.m.with four sacks of official mail."[63] *(U.S. Navy/Harry S. Truman Library)*

On a lighter note, the "war of the oranges," escalated on this trip. The banter about the origin of the orange juice on the Truman breakfast menu began on an earlier visit when, "Press Secretary Ross told newsmen of the Little White House menus, adding that Florida orange or some Florida fruit was served. Repercussions from Texas and California made it politically expedient to cut out the implied plug."[64]

It did not end there; the interstate orange juice rivalry continued in the press. The *New York Times* reported a possible solution: "A proposal had been made to install a machine in the naval station for making synthetic orange juice. Hurt Floridians are suspecting a fifth columnist from California."[65] When the news hit the amused public, others joined in. K. C. Freuby, manufacturer of the Freuby juice extractor, telegraphed Charlie Ross to tell him he was "air expressing three different models of juice extractors. So there will be no publicity involved, we are grinding off trademarks."[66]

Not to be outdone, Florida citrus growers sent some Florida oranges to the Little White House in March 1949, under the watchful eye of the Florida Highway Patrol. In a letter to Broward County Sheriff Walter Clark, the president asked the sheriff to thank all "our friends in Fort Pierce (Florida)," for sending the oranges. He then seemingly settled the debate by acknowledging in the letter, "All of us here in the Little White House now know the delicious flavor and superior merits of Florida products."[67] *(U. S. Navy/Harry S. Truman Library)*

The Key West Uniform: The Loud Shirt

"The President liked to wear colorful caps and sports shirts at Key West."[68]

(Above) Robert Wolz, executive director of the Harry S. Truman Little White House, holding one of President Truman's shirts, which was recently donated by the president's grandson, Clifton Truman Daniel.

From the end of November, and well into December 1949, the first family and a large number of staffers vacationed at the Little White House.

"Reveille and breakfast were at the convenience of the individual. Usually, lunch was served at 1 p.m., dinner at 7 p.m. Informality was the rule during meals and protocol was laid aside. About 10 a.m. each morning all hands assembled at the Little White House and left from there in a group for the beach, where they spent the forenoon. The afternoons, generally, were free for rest. The President also worked for an hour or longer most evenings after he retired to his quarters, and cleared up a backlog of official papers which he took south with him."[69]

Coming to Key West in the winter must have been a pleasurable change of pace for Truman's visitors. Guests flying to Key West to meet with the president on this trip included John Snyder, Secretary of the Treasury; and Frank Pace, Jr., Budget Director.[70]

The pleasant weather and relaxed atmosphere of Key West were conducive to holding discussions in an outdoor setting. "Under the shade of coconut and cork trees on the lawn of the winter White House on Wednesday, December 7th, the President and 16 aides held their first staff meeting on the forthcoming State of the Union message. The conference lasted one hour and forty-five minutes. It was a round table discussion devoted almost wholly to Mr. Truman's domestic program." [71]

The ever-present press was seldom disappointed. The president met with them frequently, engaging them with his famous directness.

To everyone's amusement at press conferences, the president often played the role of "Correspondent" Truman of the fictitious *Federal Register*, asking questions of his press secretary. He is playing the role here, attending one of Press Secretary Ross's press conferences during the November 1949 visit. *(U.S. Navy/Harry S. Truman Library)*

The light atmosphere at the Key West retreat was evident in the accepted dress of the day. Shortly after the presidential party arrived, everyone, from the Chief Executive on down, exchanged their stiff suits for tropical shirts. The colorful caps and bright sports shirts the president favored "came as gifts in such numbers that they spilled over into the supplies of staffers and reporters. Incoming shirts, caps, fishing gear or whatnot would be opened on a large table, where everyone was free to take his choice." What was initiated as a publicity stunt by Royal Palm Sportswear of Miami became the Key West uniform of the president, his staffers and even the newspaper reporters, and was also a source of fun. [72]

"The two great social events of the vacation at Key West were a loud shirt contest and the impersonation of the President. The Presidential assistants outdid each other in the lurid shirt deal. Bill Hassett, the kindly White House veteran, wore a pink and white check. But Matt Connolly, the President's No. 1 assistant, won hands down. A special shirt was flown in from Mexico. It was a flaming red silk with an Aztec calendar done in black and yellow."[73]

(Above left) "Loud" shirts, displayed on the lawn for selection. *(U.S. Navy/Harry S. Truman Library)* (Above right) President Truman with the press, members of the "One More Club," in their loud shirts. Always in search of the perfect photo, the press repeatedly implored, "Just one more, Mr. President," to which Truman obliged good-naturedly, giving the press the moniker "One More Club." *(U.S. Navy/Harry S.Truman Library)*

The president and his party on December 19, 1949, sporting their interpretation of the Key West uniform. Front row (l to r) Philleo Nash, Russell Andrew, (Middle row, l to r) Matthew Connolly, John Steelman, President Truman, William Hassett, Charlie Ross, (Back row, l to r) William Hopkins; David Stowe; Brig. Gen. Wallace Graham, USA; Maj. Gen. Harry Vaughn, USA; Clark Clifford; Rear Admiral Robert Dennison, USN; Brig. Gen. Robert Landry, USA; and George Elsey. *(U.S. Navy/Harry S. Truman Library)*

Wearing colorful shirts in Key West made such a lasting impression on all who visited the Little White House during the Truman era that former Truman aide Ken Hechler, seated at left, saved his loud shirt and wore it fifty years later to the welcoming reception for the participants of the Truman Legacy Symposium held at the Little White House in June 2003. Seated with him are Carol Shaughnessy from the Monroe County Tourist Development Council and Wanda Coury, former secretary to President Truman. *(Little White House Museum)*

In keeping with the casual atmosphere, picnic lunches were held on the Little White House lawn. Even in Key West, the president could not escape the formality of the White House. The all-American fare of hot dogs, hamburgers and corn on the cob was served on formal china and silver plate! (From left) John Steelman, Margaret Truman, Mrs. Truman, President Truman and an unidentified officer. *(U.S. Navy/Harry S. Truman Library)*

EIGHTH VISIT: MARCH 12-APRIL 10, 1950

More Work Than Vacation
"The task of being President never ceases for a moment"[74]
–David Lawrence

Until this visit, the president had always flown to Key West for vacations on the presidential planes, the *Sacred Cow* (C-54) or the *Independence* (DC-6), the forerunners of *Air Force One*.

(Top) President Truman arriving at Boca Chica Naval Air Station in Key West aboard the *Sacred Cow* on December 3, 1947. *(U.S. Navy/Truman Library Collection)*
(Bottom) President Truman arriving at Boca Chica Naval Air Station aboard the *Independence* on November 8, 1951. *(U.S. Navy/Harry S. Truman Library)*

On the March 1950 visit, however, the president decided to sail to Key West aboard the U.S.S. *Williamsburg*. A course was set following the coast, as it would offer smoother sailing. On March 13, 1950, near Cape Hatteras, rough seas were encountered all day. "From 3:25 p.m. on, conditions were such that it was desirable for the *Williamsburg* to proceed at two-thirds speed. The President and most members of the party stuck to their quarters all day. Attendance at meals was light."[75] Past Cape Hatteras, the seas became calm for an enjoyable sail for the rest of the trip. However, this was the last time Truman sailed to Key West.

(Top) USS *Williamsburg* in rough seas on the March 1950 trip to Key West. *(Little White House Collection)* (Bottom) USS *Williamsburg*, in calmer waters, moored at her berth in front of the Naval Administration building in Key West. *(U.S. Navy/Harry S. Truman Library Collection)*

Once the party was safely in Key West, the routine for this trip was the same as on previous visits. The naval station newspaper, the *Key West Outpost*, observed, "All during the presidential visit much time was spent signing bills, appointments and making nominations to fill government posts."[76]

"A clerical force consisting of Mr. Jack Romagna (personal stenographer to the president), Mr. E.L. Cuckenberger (White House Staff room) and Chief Yeoman Burnace L. Winkler (later relieved by Chief Yeoman Charles J. Langello) served the Presidential party. Office space was provided in the Administration Building and in building #97."[77]

When President Truman first vacationed in Key West in November 1946, a single telephone line connected Key West to the mainland. Cold War fears that the president might not be able to contact Washington, D.C., led to the installation of several additional telephone cables to route the increased activity between Key West's Little White House and the White House.

"Special telephone service was provided by a private two-positioned switchboard set up in Bldg. #97 and manned during daylight and heavy traffic hours by Miss Grace Earle and Miss Mary Crowe (of the White House Communications Staff) and at other times by Sergeants Putterman, Brown and Tarbell (of the White House Signal Center)."[78] *(U.S. Navy/Harry S. Truman Library)*

Fears over the possible loss of contact with Washington were partially realized in March 1950, when a warehouse fire in Perrine, Florida burned cables providing telephone service from the Florida Keys to the mainland. Service was disrupted for several hours. Backup service was immediately activated, and communication for the president was handled by radio teletype from the USS *Williamsburg*.[79]

The *Williamsburg* was able to provide "worldwide communications capabilities, civilian, diplomatic and military," from where it was docked along the north pier of the Navy base, just in front of the Administration Building. Retired Lt. Cmdr. Joseph C. Perry, USN, recalled his three years of duty aboard the presidential yacht where, as Chief Yoeman Perry, he prepared "a daily 12-page summary of news monitored by the sophisticated communications section of the ship from world-wide wireless transmissions." [80]

There were numerous critics who were of the opinion that the president spent too much time away from Washington. They did not know, as Admiral Dennison did, that "we had to work like hell and still not give the appearance of working, so it was really hell for all of us, but we had our regard in knowing that he (Truman) was really having a good time."[81] In reality, it mattered little whether the President was in the White House on Pennsylvania Avenue or the Little White House on Front Street as "life goes on almost exactly as it does in Washington."[82]

"The press corps is here … just as curious and persevering in representing the people's interest."[83]
(U. S. Navy/Harry S. Truman Library)

"In back of the President is an efficient staff in Washington, which sifts the important from the unimportant before sending down a pouch of mail. Anything that comes here for action is of topmost significance – and much of what is done here isn't publicized at all. The President can send for anyone and bring him here by air in a few hours for a conference. He can do business by telephone if he wishes to work faster than the airplane can carry his letters and orders."[84]

The president conferring on the Little White House lawn in November 1951 from left are : Charles Ross; President Truman; Secretary of the Treasury, John Snyder; Director of the Budget, Frank Pace; and the special counsel to the president, Clark Clifford. Not identified are the two men with their backs to the camera. *(U.S. Navy/Harry S. Truman Library)*

"President Truman has found here rest and seclusion – a chance to think through some of the major problems that bother him. He gets a vacation, of course, from the pressures of a daily calling list and from the hour-by-hour demands on his time from heads of departments and government agencies. But the task of being President never ceases for a moment."[85]

Occupying the president at this moment were difficult domestic and international issues. At home, he was, in his words, "in the midst of the most terrible struggle any President has ever had. A pathological liar from Wisconsin (Senator Joseph McCarthy) and a block-head undertaker from Nebraska (Senator Kenneth S. Wherry) are trying to ruin the bipartisan foreign policy."[86] The struggle centered on the investigative excess of McCarthyism.

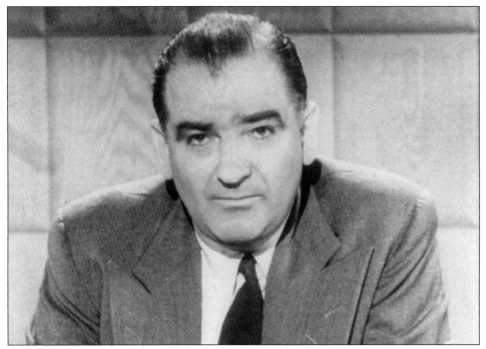

The accusations of Senator Joseph McCarthy spread fear among many in the government and throughout the nation. Eventually, his claims became so extreme that he was discredited. *(Library of Congress)*

Abroad, the Korean conflict was escalating. Intelligence reports showed "that the North Koreans were steadily continuing their buildup of forces and they were continuing to send guerrilla groups into South Korea."[87]

Then, on June 24, 1950, while at home in Independence, Missouri, Truman received a telephone call from Secretary of State Dean Acheson, informing him that the North Koreans had invaded South Korea. The Korean War had begun.[88]

MacArthur is Fired

"This was a challenge to the President under the Constitution."[89]
–Harry S. Truman, 1951

As a result of the conflict in Korea, there was heightened activity emanating from the Little White House during the March 1951 visit; there was also tighter security around it.

"Strict security was observed throughout the visit. In addition to an increased Secret Service detail about the Little White House, an armed guard was maintained around the house by the Marine Corps personnel, and a continuous watch was kept at the beach used by the President and also at adjacent Fort Taylor."[90]   *(U.S. Navy/Harry S. Truman Library)*

A guest visiting the Little White House Museum on February 23, 2003, who served as a Marine Honor Guard for President Truman at the Key West Naval Station in 1951-1952, recounted his experience while on guard at the Little White House: "Once I was posted as a guard at the door by the south porch. It was late evening and the President saw me outside. He opened the door and said the game was going to run into the night and asked me to come in and sit down. I informed the President that my Sergeant did not allow me to come in. He replied: 'Tell your Sergeant that your Commander-in-Chief ordered you to sit down.' The game lasted into the night so I was glad the President had asked me in." [91]

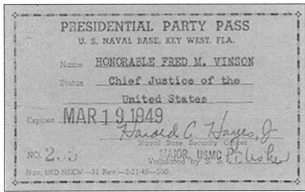

No one, not even Mrs. Truman or Chief Justice Vinson, was exempt from carrying a special pass, signed by the naval base security officer and countersigned by a representative of the Secret Service, to be permitted to enter or leave the grounds of the Little White House.[92]   *(Harry S. Truman Library)*

Guests came and went in a steady stream. On March 6, 1951, Charles E. Wilson, director of defense mobilization, flew to the Little White House to hold official briefings with the president; on March 8, W. Averell Harriman, special assistant to the president, flew in for special meetings; March 10 saw the arrival of Charles S. Murphy, special counsel to the president; then, on March 20, Eric Johnston, economic stabilization administrator, arrived at the Little White House to confer with the president and members of his staff.[93]

The president and Charles E. Wilson, director of defense mobilization, on the west lawn of the Little White House, March 6, 1951. *(U.S. Navy/Harry S. Truman Library)*

The press was filled with gloomy news of military reversals in Korea. Consumers and producers alike pushed inflation to new heights. Much of America, including former President Herbert Hoover and Joseph Kennedy, urged a return to isolationism. But Truman pushed for increased mobilization, sending American troops to both Korea under the U.N., and to Europe under NATO. Wage and price controls proved unpopular and often were perceived as unfair.[94]

Acknowledging the momentum building against him, the president revealed his perspective on how he hoped to be judged by history at a press conference held on the north lawn of the Little White House on March 15, 1951: "All any president can do is endeavor to make the executive branch of government run in an efficient manner," Truman said in response to a question. "No president can be evaluated," he added, "during his term in office or during the 25 years after it. That takes a projected survey." When asked what he believed the legacy of his administration would be, he said, "I hope that it will be remembered for its sincere effort for world peace. If we accomplish that and get through this era without a third world war, that will be what it will be remembered for." [95]

President Truman holding a press conference on March 18, 1951 on the Little White House lawn. *(Little White House Museum)*

Truman's self-assessment was prophetic. During the 1952 presidential campaign, as a result of such issues as the war in Korea and the economic crisis at home, only twenty-three percent of the country approved of the way he was handling his job.[96]

Interestingly, in the light of history, the public's perception of President Truman has changed considerably. In a poll ranking U. S. presidents in areas that included crisis leadership, moral authority, civil rights, national relations, public persuasion, and overall performance conducted in 2000 by C-Span Cable Network at the conclusion of a year-long series entitled "Presidential Life Portraits," President Truman was ranked 5th. Only Lincoln, Franklin Roosevelt, Washington and Theodore Roosevelt ranked higher.

Behind the prevailing pessimistic atmosphere, a ray of hope appeared in Korea. General Matthew Ridgway's artillery offensive gained some positive ground for the Allied forces. Truman staffers, the Pentagon and the State Department felt the time was right to prepare a cease-fire proposal. On March 20, 1951, from the Little White House, Truman submitted a draft proposal calling for a cease-fire to the other seventeen U.N. member nations with troops in Korea. The essence of this proposal was sent to General MacArthur, World War II hero and the Allied commander in Korea, via telegram on that same day, advising him that "strong UN feeling persists that further diplomatic effort towards settlement should be made before any advance with major forces north of 38th parallel. Time will be required to determine diplomatic reactions and permit new negotiations that may develop." [97]

General Douglas MacArthur and President Truman met on Wake Island on October 10, 1950 to discuss what the "official" Korea policy would be. *(US Navy/Harry S. Truman Library)*

General MacArthur had a reputation for issuing inflammatory declarations from the front lines and, in an effort to control the general's power-grabbing tactics, the meeting on Wake Island was held. The understanding was reached that any policy statements would be issued by Washington.

Despite this agreement, on March 23, 1951, General MacArthur seized the initiative with his own statement: "The enemy, therefore, must by now be painfully aware that a decision of the United States to depart from its tolerant effort to contain the war to the areas of Korea, through an expansion of our military operations to his coastal areas and interior bases, would doom Red China to the risk of imminent military collapse."[98]

MacArthur's statement, conflicting with the presidential directive, prompted President Truman to relieve him of his command in Korea and replace him with General Ridgeway.

Truman's perspective on his decision is clearly stated in his book, *Memoirs*: "It was an act totally disregarding all directives to abstain from any declarations on foreign policy. It was an open defiance of my orders as President and as Commander in Chief. This was a challenge to the President under the Constitution. It also flouted the policy of the United Nations."[99]

Americans, however, could not believe Truman relieved this popular World War hero of his command. The country was in an uproar, with cries for impeachment coming from every corner. Telegrams poured into the White House. People resorted to any means to voice their opinions: "In Charleston, Maryland, a woman was told that she couldn't send a wire to the White House calling the President a moron; she and the clerk riffled through a Roget's thesaurus until they found the acceptable 'wilting.'" Members of Congress, too, were inundated by telegrams from angry constituents, all expressing variations of the same theme: "Impeach the Judas in the White House who sold us down the river to the left wingers and the UN." [100]

The president stood firm. Former Secretary of State Dean Rusk later explained Truman's decision this way: "I am convinced that 95 percent of Truman's decision to fire MacArthur hinged on the relationship of the president as the Commander in Chief to his general and on civilian control of the military." [101]

Perhaps he was guided in his decision by a handwritten note by fellow Missourian, Mark Twain, kept on his White House desk, "Always do right. This will gratify some people and astonish the rest."

A Key West Thanksgiving

"Jumbo Shrimp cocktails, Roast Turkey with chestnut-oyster dressing and giblet gravy, cranberry sauce, candied sweet potatoes, creamed green peas, Parker House rolls, strawberry preserves, assorted cheeses and crackers, mince and pumpkin pies, plum pudding, fruit cake, and mixed nuts, mints, candies and chocolates. Fruit punch and demitasse." [102]

It had been the custom of the first family to celebrate the holidays, whenever possible, in Independence, Missouri, with Mrs. Truman's mother, Mrs. Wallace. An exception to this ritual was Thanksgiving, on November 22, 1951, which was enjoyed in the Little White House.

The Thanksgiving feast was prepared by the Filipino stewards assigned to the *Williamsburg*. They were responsible for all meals served at the Little White House, often delivering them from the ship by steam tray, and were "capable of putting on elaborate meals required for diplomats and visitors of state." Their presentation was exquisite; "no one ever saw a radish; it was always a rosette." [103]

Stewards from the USS *Williamsburg* standing by the Thanksgiving table at the Little White House (*U. S. Navy/Little White House Museum*)

The Little White House dining room table set for the 1951 Key West Thanksgiving dinner. *(U.S. Navy/Harry S. Truman Library)*

Chief Justice Frederick M. Vinson and Mrs. Vinson leaving the Little White House for their return to Washington after having joined the Trumans for the Key West Thanksgiving dinner. *(U.S. Navy/Harry S. Truman Library)*

Still smarting from the criticism leveled at him for his frequent vacations, Truman wrote to his friend, Carl Hatch, United States District Court judge, on November 29, 1951: "I have been extremely busy. The papers refer to this visit down here as a vacation. The only thing that would in any way make it look as if it were a vacation is the fact that I do not have a steady stream of visitors all day long and can sit down and get through my document list and catch up with correspondence." [104]

Decisions were made that only he, as president, could make: "Never a day goes by that I do not have to make some decision which affects the whole of the United States and sometimes the rest of the world. I had one of that sort to make yesterday." [105]

On this trip, the Joint Chiefs of Staff arrived in Key West to confer with Truman on war strategy, and to "dispel rumors that peace was at hand."[106] The president also held budget-planning sessions and planned for his State of the Union address.

President Truman working on the budget under the palms on Little White House front lawn on December 6, 1951. On the left is Mr. W. F. McCandless with the Bureau of Budgets; on the right is Mr. F. J. Lawton, Director of the Budget. *(U.S. Navy/Harry S. Truman Library)*

Regular staff meetings, like this one on Dec. 3, 1951, were held on the lawns of the Little White House. *(U.S. Navy/Harry S. Truman Library)*

Truman: Civil Rights Champion

Civil rights action was also on the president's agenda on this trip. He had been ineffective in moving civil rights reform through Congress, where southern Democrats suffocated the proposed legislation. He vowed, however, to continue "asking for equal opportunity for all human beings and, as long as I am here, I am going to continue that fight."[107]

Truman circumvented Congress to achieve his civil rights objectives through the use of executive orders. On December 3, 1951, from the Little White House, he issued Executive Order #10308, requiring federal contractors to hire blacks and other minorities.[108]

Prior to this, he convened the first Civil Rights Commission. He was the first president to address the NAACP, which he did on June 29, 1947. In July 1948, he issued two important executive orders impacting civil rights: Executive Order #9981, desegregating the U.S. military, and Executive Order #9982, desegregating the federal workforce.

In the forward to Michael R. Gardner's book, *Harry Truman & Civil Rights – Moral Courage & Political Risks*, Kweisi Mfume, current president and CEO of the NAACP, lauds Truman's efforts: "Truman knew his actions could end his chances to be elected president and further capture the Democratic Party. Yet in the midst of danger and controversy, he remained undeterred in his fight for equality and justice for all citizens." [109]

President Truman's stance on civil rights, evidenced by the landmark decisions he made, has prompted many to regard him as the greatest proponent of civil rights since Abraham Lincoln. In Kweisi Mfume's words, "President Truman's bravery and dogged determination opened many doors and forever changed the course of history." [110]

In tribute to Harry Truman's forward-thinking stance on civil rights, presidential scholars and distinguished guests attending the second annual Truman Legacy Symposium in Key West in May 2004 discussed and analyzed the impact of this critical aspect of his legacy.

"Trying to Make Up his Mind." Karl Kae Knecht, the *Evansville Indiana Courier (1952)*. *(Evansville Courier/Harry S. Truman Library)*

With the Democratic nominating convention coming up in the early fall of 1952, speculation was running rampant in the press: Would Truman run for a second term?

In fact, his mind really was made up. "In mid-November 1951, during a brief vacation in Key West, Truman gathered (his senior staff members) about the poker table on the porch at the Little White House to read aloud the statement he had written on April 12, 1950, and that he planned to release in the coming spring, in April 1952, well in advance of the Democratic National Convention. He was not running again; but for the next five months, he cautioned them, there must be utmost secrecy. He was only telling them now, he explained, so they could start making their own plans." [111]

It is believed that no staff member ever leaked this information. The speculative articles continued.

The Final Presidential Visit
"You fellows are all trying to set a date for me to
announce but I'll set the date myself." [112]
–Harry S. Truman, 1952

Truman's last visit to the Little White House as president included the usual eagerly anticipated swimming and fishing, but the level of work was intense and speculation surrounding Truman's decision whether or not to run again dominated the visit.

"On the sands of Key West…" Gib Crockett, March 18, 1952. *(Original pencil and ink drawing in collection of Little White House Museum.)*

The "startling" write-in vote in Minnesota for General Dwight D. Eisenhower, and Truman's loss to Estes Kefauver of Tennessee in New Hampshire's primary for delegates to the Democratic National Convention, only heightened the speculation. [113]

At a press conference held at the press headquarters across from the Little White House on March 20, 1952, President Truman "parried questions with an appearance of tired patience." [114]   *(U. S. Navy/Harry S. Truman Library)*

In the press, he "emphatically disavowed predictions of his party's National Chairman that his decision on whether to seek re-election would depend on whether peace was reached in Korea. He maintained a steady "no comment" on his future plans." [115]

On March 29, 1952, two days after his return to Washington from the Little White House, Truman ended speculation when he declared, "I shall not be a candidate for re-election. I have served my country long and I think, efficiently and honestly. I shall not accept a re-nomination. I do not feel that it is my duty to spend another four years in the White House." [116]

Much to the dismay of the people of Key West, this announcement also marked the end of Truman's years in residence in the island city.

Post Presidential Visits

"We are anxious to get back for more Key West sunshine" [117]
–Bess Truman, 1968

Following his presidency, Truman returned to the Florida Keys and Key West on several occasions, although he never again stayed in the Little White House. In his role as a private citizen, he felt he was entitled to no special privileges, and chose instead to stay with his local friends, the John Spottswood family. However, when visiting Key West, the former commander in chief always paid his respects to the base commander.

His first trip back to the Keys, to both Islamorada and Key West, was February 9-28, 1957.

During this visit the former president and Mrs. Truman, along with John and Mary Spottswood, dined at the Little White House on February 23, 1957, as guests of Rear Admiral Francis McCorkle and Mrs. McCorkle. *(U.S. Navy/Harry S. Truman Library)*

(Above) In February 1957, Truman was the guest of honor at a fundraising dinner to benefit the Truman Library held at Key West's Casa Marina Hotel, where over $10,000 was raised. Seated from left: Mary Spottswood, Harry Truman, John Spottswood, Bess Truman, US Senator Spessard Holland, Florence Spottswood, and unidentified guest. (*Little White House Collection*) (Below) Truman signed the fundraising dinner menu cover for John Spottswood's young son, John, Jr., to whom Truman referred as Jack. (*Courtesy Spottswood Family Collection*)

HARRY S. TRUMAN

May Jack Spottswood have a long, happy life and be a good man. Harry Truman

Three years later, in February 1960, the Trumans again vacationed in Florida, primarily in Miami. They made a quick side trip to Key West from February 23rd through the 25th, during which time they visited the Little White House as guests of Rear Admiral Lloyd M. Mustin. [118]

Mrs. Truman signing the guest book at the Little White House in February 1960. Looking on from left are Admiral Mustin, John Spottswood and Harry Truman. *(U.S. Navy/Harry S. Truman Library)*

Four more years passed before the former president and Mrs. Truman again chose to vacation in Florida. In March 1964, they flew to Florida, staying on Duck Key for most of the vacation. The Trumans, accompanied by their daughter, Margaret, her husband, Clifton Daniel, and their two children, also visited Key West. The family spent time with the Spottswoods, and the former president paid his respects to Rear Admiral Lewis J. Kirn at the Little White House on March 23, 1964. [119]

The Truman family at the Little White House on March 23, 1964. Margaret Truman Daniel is on the left, Mrs. Truman is the fourth woman from left, Senator John Spottswood is in the dark suit, and Margaret's husband, Clifton Daniel, is to the right of Senator Spottswood. The two boys are the Truman grandchildren, Clifton Truman Daniel on the left and William Daniel on the right. *(Photograph by Jack Burke/ Little White House Museum)*

Inside the Little White House, Admiral Kirn had a surprise waiting for the former president – his piano, last seen on the de-commissioned USS *Williamsburg*. During his efforts to restore the Little White House to its Truman-era appearance, Admiral Kirn had asked the Navy to conduct a diligent search for Truman's piano. After many months of searching, it was located in storage in a Navy warehouse in Bremerton, Washington. Once it was found, Charles Robinson, who built President Truman's poker table and was still employed in the base cabinet shop, restored the piano for Admiral Kirn.[120]

Truman played for Admiral Kirn and the assembled guests. The piano is still in place in the living room of the Little White House Museum. *(U.S. Navy/Monroe County Public Library)*

Truman toured the base on the 1964 trip, here in the company of Senator John Spottswood. *(U. S. Navy/Harry S. Truman Library)*

The tour of the base in March 1964 also included a visit to the U. S. Naval School for Underwater Swimmers. In this photo, Lt. j.g. K. Gibble introduces Underwater Swimmers instructors (front row) to Mr. Truman, with past graduate Senator John M. Spottswood looking on. Mr. Truman is pictured greeting Eugene A. Cahill, Shipfitter First Class. In rank behind the instructors stands the class. *(U. S. Navy/Harry S. Truman Library)*

The Truman family again vacationed in Key West in March 1968. The former president, Mrs. Truman, their daughter Margaret, son-in-law Clifton Daniel, and their grandchildren stayed in Key West in a private villa at the Casa Marina, owned by Senator Spottswood.

On this visit, Truman held a press conference on March 20, 1968. The frailties of advancing age had diminished neither his candor nor his humor. His short, no-frills answers to questions, peppered with his characteristic directness, reflected the character of the plain-spoken man from Missouri.

The answer to a question about whether he worried at night about his decision to drop the atomic bomb on Japan brought out his "buck stops here" attitude: "No, I sleep very well every night. I don't have any trouble because when I make a statement it is what I believe and I don't have to remember it because I will answer it the same way next time you ask." [121]

The answer to a question about his apparent loss of weight showed that he had not lost his humor nor his ability to poke fun at himself. "Well," he candidly asserted, "I lost a little weight immediately after I got out of the White House. I had it coming, I was too fat just like all of these men in high places, they eat too much." [122]

The final words of the press conference spoke volumes about the Truman unpretentiousness. At the conclusion of the press conference, as he was walking away, he turned to the assembled press and said, "I want to tell you I appreciated the fact you wanted a press conference of me and I am very happy about it." [123]

In thanking Mrs. John Spottswood for her hospitality on the March 1968 visit, Mrs. Truman wrote in May 1968, "Never have we had such a wonderful vacation as we did on our trip to Key West. We are anxious to get back for more Key West sunshine."[124] The following year, in April 1969, at almost eighty-five years of age, a frail Harry Truman returned to Key West for what would be the last time.

Former President Truman autographing photographs in April 1969 in John Spottswood's office, with Spottswood looking on. *(Monroe County Public Library)*

Advancing age did not keep Truman from the proprieties of protocol. On April 3, 1969, the former president visited the Little White House to pay his respects to Rear Admiral Frederick J. Brush. His famous cane, so long an integral part of his attire, was now used for stability. *(Monroe County Public Library)*

Throughout the span of President Truman's visits, his presence focused international attention on Key West. His choice to return again and again gave the unpretentious "frame dwelling" on the small island in the Straits of Florida a special place in history.

CHAPTER FOUR

Key West is "Trumanized"
The Man from Missouri Meets the Key West Conchs

Harry S. Truman's visits to Key West not only put the island on the international map, they also brought about an economic boom and left a distinctly personal impression on its people. Notably, fifty years after he left office, Truman's legacy in Key West lives on.

Today, visitors and locals alike have but to travel into Old Town via Truman Avenue to be reminded of the unique connection between this president and the island community. Guests who visit the Little White House Museum experience firsthand the atmosphere that Truman and his staff found so appealing in the Key West presidential retreat. The selection of Key West as the site for the peace talks between Azerbaijan and Armenia held at the Little White House in April 2000, and for the scholarly Truman Legacy Symposium held in June each year, perpetuates the ongoing legacy of this important president.

However, when Truman first arrived, with the exception of a few headline-grabbing events of national or international importance, Key West was an insular, close-knit community with a limited exposure to national politics.

The locals had grown accustomed to the comings and goings of the Navy. They knew Navy expansion meant prosperous times and more contact with the outside world; Navy downsizing meant relying once again on island ingenuity and resourcefulness.

The character of these island people, collectively referred to as Conchs, was shaped by their maritime history and their limited access to the world. They were self-reliant island people, used to making do with what they had. Watching "outsiders" come and go made them independent and protective of the island ways. Living in relative isolation, always subject to the whims of nature, made them patient and resourceful. Generations of families living at close quarters in small places created a people that, while knowing everything about everybody, respected privacy.

Such were the Conchs encountered by President Truman in the mid 1940s, and they are little different today. Regardless of the underlying motivation behind the choice of Key West for Harry Truman's first visit, his reason for returning so often during his presidency, and five times after he left office, was perhaps simply because the plain spoken man from Missouri felt comfortable among the Key West Conchs. To Paul Sher, who owned a jewelry store on Duval Street throughout the Truman era, the reason was obvious: "He liked it here and nobody bothered him! He could walk down the street and nobody would rush up to him and say 'May I have your autograph' or anything like that."[1]

President Truman receiving best wishes on behalf of the city from City Manager David King. Mayor John Carbonell is looking on with an unidentified Boy Scout. *(US Navy/Harry S. Truman Library)*

Whatever the reason — the character of the locals, the weather, or the isolation — Truman felt at ease in Key West. During a gathering of three former Truman staff members, all octogenarians, participating in the 2003 Truman Legacy Symposium, George Elsey, former special assistant to President Truman, offered this perspective: "Truman did not have all the intrusion he had in Washington."[2] Former Truman aide Ken Hechler recalled the "relaxed circumstances in Key West," and while there was "lots of work on the Key West vacations, Truman was in a much better mood while in Key West."[3]

Just as Truman benefited from the island atmosphere, there is no doubt the Key West community benefited substantially. The most significant impact of the arrival of President Truman in Key West was to place it in the world's spotlight for five years.

Paul Wilder of the *Tampa Daily Tribune* described the ripple effect of the presidential visits in an article written on December 2, 1951: "The southernmost Florida city for several weeks is the nerve center of the world — It's the temporary capital of the United States. Airplanes fly in and out daily with pouches containing some of the nation's most important policy documents. Telephone lines and cables carry conversations on matters that not only affect the livelihood of every citizen of the U.S., but may affect the future, one way or another, of people all over the globe. Telegraph wire strung along the Overseas Highway linking Key West with the Florida mainland carry the news of the doings here to newspapers and radio stations in all parts of the world. Moving pictures shot here in the last few days are being viewed in movie theaters and television sets by countless millions. All this because one man decided to spend his vacation here — and that man is the president of the United States."

By choosing to vacation in Key West, President Truman became its biggest promoter of tourism. Eagerly anticipating the first visit, Harold Laubcher of the chamber of commerce acknowledged the potential impact of hosting this famous guest: "As a result of President Truman coming here for a week, giving Key West nationwide publicity, additional hundreds of persons from all over the country are likely to be here during the 1946-47 winter season."[4]

In fact, the entire state benefited from Truman's vacation choice. Incoming tourists had to drive the entire length of Florida to reach Key West. Roy Beckman of the Florida Advertising Commission had this advice: "Want to put your city on the map? Mr. Truman is doing (it) for Key West…. By selecting Key West as his vacation home, President Truman has given Florida thousands of dollars worth of publicity".[5]

The economic impact of the repeated presidential visits cannot be underestimated. The free publicity that brought additional tourists was a boon to local businesses. "Key West, enjoying its best tourist season since the end of the war, gave a warm welcome to the man they credit with putting this southernmost United States town on the map."[6]

Hotel occupancy increased: "Max Marmonstein, owner of the Casa Marina Hotel, the swankiest in town, is operating his hostelry three weeks early because of 'very heavy' tourist demand, and J. D. McAndrews, manager of the year-round La Concha Hotel, says business has risen steadily since Mr. Truman came to town."[7] Increased tourism aside, the mere presence of the support staff and newsmen traveling on expense accounts increased hotel and guest cottage occupancy and filled restaurants to capacity. Local restaurants stocked more expensive wine, cigars, and cuts of meat when they knew so many more urbane visitors would be coming. "Shopkeepers in America's 'farthest south' city are frank to say, regardless of their personal opinions of the Fair Deal, that the President has meant more for the local economy than sailfishing or sunny beaches. With the annual visits he began five years ago, tourist cash and Navy pay have run a cheerful stream into the tills of Key West business."[8]

Despite the heightened activity brought about by the president being in town, Washington made it clear that there would be no official local duties for him to perform while in Key West: "As the trip to Key West had been planned solely for rest and relaxation, the local officials had been asked specifically not to plan any official entertainment or receptions for the President."[9] As was the island way, the locals gave the Truman a wide berth, minding their own business.

It did not take very long, however, for President Truman to catch the island spirit. Moments after arriving at the Little White House, the first order of the day for the president was to change from the stiff Washington suit into a tropical shirt with khaki slacks and a golf cap with long visor or a pith helmet. Some other hats even came complete with attached sunglasses.[10]

Once free of urban confines, Truman set out to do what most people vacationing in Key West do: he swam and he walked. These were his two favorite forms of exercise, and Key West was conducive to both.

A typical day in Key West began with the president "downstairs by seven in the morning for a shot of bourbon, which always astonished the Filipino (steward), a glass of orange juice, then a long walk accompanied by a Secret Service agent, and on rare occasions by a member of his staff who by strange chance happened to be up that early."[11]

Mr. Truman liked to walk each morning, and did so "at his old Army pace of 120 steps per minute."[12] When out walking, the president always carried a cane, not necessarily for stability, but as a fashion accessory. As a former haberdasher, he viewed the cane as part of his walking attire.

In casual clothes, complete with his signature pith helmet and cane, the president departs for a walk on November 29, 1949, with, from left, Admiral Robert Dennison, USN; General Harry Vaughn, USA; Margaret Truman; John Steelman; and David DeLloyd. *(U.S. Navy/Harry S. Truman Library)*

Normally Truman confined his walking to the base, which provided security and privacy. Once, while walking around the base, he stopped in at the enlisted men's mess, "lined up with the men, waited his turn, and enjoyed the meal. This visit took everyone by surprise."[13]

Occasionally on his walks, Truman ventured into town, usually in the company of a small handful of Secret Service agents. These excursions led to encounters with locals and sparked lasting memories. As the frequency of the walks about town increased, there was a very human outcome: the man from Missouri responded warmly to Conch hospitality, and the citizens of Key West responded in kind.

Many of the local stories of Truman in Key West come from the recollections of a few local, or once local, people who remember the past. It is from their memories that an oral history has been compiled. To them is owed a deep gratitude for these recollections that give life to historic facts. Individual memories, colored as they are by personal perspective and by the passage of time, are an invaluable component of the history of the island, adding richness and vibrancy to the tapestry of the past.

On one of Truman's walks about town, documented by the *Miami Herald*, local restaurateur Sebastian Cabrera offered the president and his entourage a cup of coffee as they walked by his restaurant. The president said he would take a rain check. The Secret Service returned later to check out Carbrera's Caribe Restaurant on Front Street, and soon after, "the door opened and in walked a grinning customer in a green billed fishing cap and colorful sport shirt. 'I'm here,' said the President as he climbed up on a counter stool, 'to get that cup of coffee you promised me.' The President paid Sebastian with an autographed one-dollar bill. 'This ought to be a profitable cup of coffee,' the President told Sebastian, 'because a lot of people think this signature is valuable.'"[14] The framed dollar was displayed for years in the restaurant until a late-night robbery claimed it. The coffee cup was donated to the local historical society.

The president dropped in unexpectedly on local establishments with some frequency. Harry Knight, until recently Monroe County tax collector, remembers the day the lively chatter in his family's restaurant on Duval Street suddenly fell silent as the group of locals gathered there noticed that they were being joined by the President of the United States. Obviously concerned that he had disturbed their camaraderie, Truman told everyone to resume what they were doing. Everyone did. Treating him as though he were one of their own, the locals resumed their conversations.[15]

With a memory as vivid as though it were yesterday, Minnie Estevez recalls the morning she and her husband, Ralph, were walking on Duval Street when the president, wearing a bright flowered shirt, turned onto Duval from Southard Street and bumped into them. The couple immediately recognized him, and Ralph said, "Good morning, Mr. President," to which he replied, "Good morning, son." With the memory lighting up her face, Miss Minnie recalls the president turning to her and saying, "Good morning," before proceeding on his way. To this day Miss Minnie says she will always remember his beautiful smile.[16]

On March 17, 1952, on his last visit as president, Truman and Judge Roy Harper, accompanied by the Secret Service, went for a walk into town. "The President noticed that the aquarium was being opened for the day, so he and Judge Harper went in and were shown around by the manager, Mr. Bill Kroll. The President saw some baby sea horses which had just hatched, a permit fish, porcupine fish and a 500-lb. loggerhead turtle, all natives of the waters that surround Key West."[17]

Swimming was another favorite pastime. Beaches in the Keys are few, as the outlying coral reef formations do not allow for much coastal sand buildup. In order to accommodate the president, a perfect swimming spot was created on a sandy spit of land lying in a protected area on the base, not far from the Little White House. "Normally there wasn't much sand on this or other Key West beaches, but the Navy always hauled or pumped or somehow got sand for the President's beach. The crushed coral that is natural there scratches the feet."[18] A wooden structure was converted into a cabana, and palm trees and colorful oleander bushes were planted to give it a real tropical ambiance. A concrete shuffleboard was also installed.[19]

The naming of this beach was the first indication of the effect the president was having on the island: "Many things in Key West are being 'Trumanized.' It was 10 A.M. when the President set out for the Truman Beach – which not so long ago was prosaically called the enlisted men's beach."[20]

Truman Beach became a favorite gathering spot for the presidential party. On his recent visit to Key West, former aide Ken Hechler had one request: to be able to swim off a beach that would duplicate the experience of 50 years ago. With the president's beach long ago filled in by the Navy, a sampling of several of Key West's beaches did not produce a single one that could even begin to measure up to the wonderful swimming spot of his memories.[21]

(Above) Aerial view of Truman Beach and the presidential cabana. Beach volleyball was enjoyed in the sand behind the cabana. (*U.S. Navy/Harry S. Truman Library*)

(Below) The president and his staff relaxing at Truman Beach in March 1950. Standing from left: Dr. John R. Steelman, Richard E. Neustadt, Donald S. Dawson, Milton P. Kayle, Russell P. Andrews. Seated from left: Ken Hechler, Dallas C. Halverstadt, Major General Harry H. Vaughan, President Truman, and David M. Noyes. (*Paul Begley/ Harry S. Truman Library*)

The presidential party relaxing at Truman Beach with President Truman, wearing the cap and seated on the wall. Civil War-era Fort Zachary Taylor is in the background. *(U.S. Navy/Harry S. Truman Library)*

The president strategizing with Frank E. McKinney, chairman of the Democratic National Committee, on the seawall at Truman Beach on March 18, 1952. *(U. S. Navy/Harry S. Truman Library)*

The visits to Truman Beach were relaxing events despite the occasional large fish sightings: "As President Truman was finishing his swim and wading ashore in water up to his knees, someone hollered out: 'Barracuda'! The president, and everyone else, left quickly. No one is certain it was a barracuda but Key West natives were disturbed at that report, saying barracudas wouldn't come in that close unless they were following something shiny or metallic. Conchs didn't like tourists to think their waters were unsafe. A large fish was observed. One secret service guard took a swing at it with an oar but missed. No one really knows what kind of fish it was."[22]

Another favorite pastime among staff and guests was sport fishing, for which Key West is famous. The president seemed to enjoy fishing best when doing it vicariously, putting a line in the water only on occasion. Even then, recalls Wesley Saunders, son of then submarine base commander, Captain Willard Saunders, Truman was "fully assisted at fishing." [23]

Wesley Saunders is in a position to know. As a young man of thirteen, and called Bill at the time, he had the occasion to fish with the president and has a memento to prove it. It was a school day on November 22, 1946, and Admiral Leahy, the president's naval aide, was discussing a fishing trip with Bill's father. As fathers are inclined to do, he asked the admiral if young Bill could go along.

Bill was invited, and much to his surprise, the president and his party boarded a destroyer and headed out at full speed to the Dry Tortugas, some 70 miles away, to meet up with the boat that was to take them fishing. Wesley recalls that while the party fished off the fishing boat, the destroyer circled some distance away. Returning to Key West on the destroyer, he remembers the president joined him as he stood in his favorite spot towards the ship's bow.[24]

There is more to the story. As they stood together, young Bill confided in the president that since he had missed school to go on this fishing trip, he would need an excuse to present to the principal the following day. He recalls Truman responded by calling out, "Get a pad!" One was brought to him, a sailor handed him a pen, and he promptly penned out the excuse.[25]

President Truman with Wesley "Bill" Saunders on a destroyer, returning to Key West from fishing off the Dry Tortugas. According to Wesley Saunders, he is not pointing at anything in particular. When the president joined him, a photographer saw a photo opportunity and posed the shot.[26] (*U.S. Navy/Harry S. Truman Library*)

Note written by President Truman on behalf of Wesley "Bill" Saunders. Mr. Saunders also recalls having the note almost thrown away when he presented it to the principal, Horace O'Bryant. Mr. O'Bryant had given the note a cursory glance, thinking it was from Bill's parents. Bill had the presence of mind to ask for it back. Only then did Mr. O'Bryant realize the identity of its author.[27] (*Courtesy Wesley Saunders*)

Nov. 27, 1946

Mrs. O'Brien:—

Please excuse Bill Saunders for his absence from school today. I needed him for a fishing guide.

Respectfully,

Harry S. Truman

There were other simple pleasures President Truman could enjoy on the small island whose people respected his privacy. One that is rather extraordinary for a sitting president was his freedom to drive around the island and even up the Keys which, by his own account, was much to his pleasure: "I had taken our fancy open car and drove up the famous Key West causeway (US 1) 40 minutes to see what it looked like. It was a great engineering feat and a lovely drive. It is a toll road and we almost scared the men at the first tollgate to death when we drove up."[28]

The President of the United States at the wheel of a car in Key West on December 13, 1949. *(U.S. Navy/Harry S. Truman Collection)*

While in Key West, Truman attended church services at either the base chapel or at various churches in town. The relaxed Key West atmosphere even extended to matters of faith, as the time and location of which service to attend were apparently last-minute decisions. In March 1949, he wrote to Mrs. Truman that he and Judge Vinson (Chief Justice Frederick M. Vinson) were "debating whether to go to church at eleven o'clock and then go to the beach or go to the beach at ten and hope to get to church later or some other day. The latter will probably do."[29]

A child's baptism at the base chapel, by coincidence witnessed by the president, was recalled by CWO Donald Cree, USN (Ret), during his visit to the Little White House Museum on February 22, 2002. Written in the Little White House Guest Journal is his recollection of the event: "While serving as a SOM1 at the Fleet Sonar School (I) had an occasion to attend church services at the Base Chapel as my son, Donald Bruce, was christened while the President sat in the pews. I received the following day, on the USS *Williamsburg* an autographed Church Program signed by the President and wishing my son 'Best of Luck.'"[30]

President Truman being greeted by Protestant Chaplain, Lieutenant Harold Menges, USN, upon leaving the Key West Naval Station chapel on March 18, 1951. *(U.S. Navy/Harry S. Truman Library)*

While in Key West, the president made a personal donation of $100 to the new memorial chapel that was being constructed at the Naval Station for the purchase of the altar cloth, pulpit hangings and Bible marker.[31]

When Mrs. Truman and Margaret were in town, the president attended Mass with them at St. Paul's Episcopal Church on Duval Street. Mary Sweeting Breedlove and Mary Anne Matchett, St. Paul parishioners, recalled the "stir" in church when the First Family attended the 11 o'clock service.[32]

In March 1947, Truman, shown here with the Reverend J. C. Yelton, paid a surprise visit to Key West's First Baptist Church, where he heard a sermon on peace of mind. "The pastor had only 10 minutes notice and the majority of the congregation was unaware of his presence until after the benediction."[33] (*U.S. Navy/Harry S. Truman Library*)

An appearance of lasting impression was memorialized in the 1960 Key West High School yearbook. In a never-again-repeated milestone for the local high school, a United States president spoke to the students. The fact that Truman had been out of office for a few years did not lessen the impact nor diminish the awe felt by the students, family and guests assembled in the packed, standing-room-only auditorium.

Former President Truman entering Key West High School with John Spottswood. *(Courtesy 1960 Key West High School Yearbook)*

Former President Truman being escorted into the Key West High School auditorium by Superintendent of Public Instruction Horace O'Bryant on February 24, 1960. *(Courtesy 1960 Key West High School Yearbook)*

Ed Swift, now president of Historic Tours of America, Inc., remembers that day, feeling respect and pride as he sat in the auditorium as a high school freshman. He recalls experiencing the famous Truman directness when, at the conclusion of his speech, the former president said that he would take questions from the students, but that they needed to know up front, "If you ask a smart-aleck question, you'll get a 'smart-aleck answer.'" But that never happened, recalls Swift, as the teachers had spent time preparing their students for this important visit.[34] The students made Key West proud. According to the yearbook, Truman "appeared to be favorably impressed by Key West High School."[35]

During each presidential visit, a highlight for locals was to watch Truman's motorcade as it traveled through town from the naval air base at Boca Chica to the Little White House. Eager to catch a glimpse of their famous visitor, they lined the streets along the entire route.

Eugene Roberts remembers an honor he received in 1951 when he was Key West High School senior class president. In an unforgettable experience initiated by Truman family friend John Spottswood, Eugene was selected to represent the student body to greet President Truman upon his arrival at Boca Chica, and to ride in the motorcade with him through the streets of Key West to the Little White House.[36]

President Truman acknowledging the Key West crowd out to greet him at the corner of Duval and Division Street on February 20, 1948. *(U. S. Navy/Harry S. Truman Little White House)*

School children lined up in front of Division Street Elementary School to welcome the president. Mary Sweeting Breedlove and Anne Matchett, who attended the elementary school at the time, remember "how patriotic we all felt during those times, with flags and bands playing."[37] *(U. S. Navy/Harry S. Truman Library)*

The welcoming and the curious turned out to greet the president at the corner of Duval and Southard streets. Truman responded to the reception in a letter to the Key West mayor, Maitland Adams: "Please accept from a grateful heart this assurance of my appreciation to the wonderful welcome accorded to me by yourself and the good people of Key West and community."[38] *(U.S. Navy/Harry S. Truman Library)*

Throngs of Key West citizens lined the president's route through town on March 7, 1952. Out of respect for the stature of their famous visitor, many women donned hats. *(Courtesy Percy Curry)*

Current Key West City Commissioner Merili McCoy recalls the day a group of local teenagers "crashed" the presidential motorcade as a prank. In a car driven by Bessie Knowles, a group of Key West High School students, dismissed from school specifically to attend the parade, decided it would be more fun to be in the parade than to watch it and slipped into Truman's motorcade as it was headed down Division Street.[39] *(Courtesy Percy Curry)*

Mayor Emeritus of Monroe County Wilhelmina Harvey, wife of then-mayor of Key West, C. B. Harvey, meeting President Truman in 1951.

The First Family happened to be in Key West during the taking of the 1950 census. Local Navy wife and census volunteer Eileen Nolte was assigned the base, and with it, its famous part-time resident. Everyone found humor in the standardized questions asked of President Truman, which included, "Is this your permanent address," and "What is your occupation." *(U. S. Navy/Harry S. Truman Library)*

Key West showed its pride in the presidential visitor by finding ways to honor him. On occasion, President Truman also graciously took the time to accept the various honors bestowed upon him.

In 1949, by action of the City Commission, Division Street, down which the president's motorcade traveled, was renamed Truman Avenue. Margaret Street, at the intersection of Truman Avenue is, by pleasant coincidence, the name of Truman's daughter. The Monroe County School Board also renamed Division Street School Truman Elementary School. *(U. S. Navy/Harry S. Truman Library)*

On November 9, 1948, the American Legion presented Truman with a gold medal, commemorating his earlier visit to the American Legion National Convention in Miami, and with three guayaberas, Cuban-made linen sports shirts. From left, Vance Stirrup, commander 10th district of Florida; Albert Mills, past national committeeman; and George A. Warren, post commander.[40] *(U. S. Navy/Harry S. Truman Library)*

On December 3, 1949, two ceremonies were held on the Little White House lawn. In the first presentation, Truman was made honorary life member and past grand master of the Grand Lodge of Free and Accepted Masons of Florida. In accepting this honorary membership, he told the assembled group: "This is indeed a highly appreciated honor you have conferred on me. It is one that a man seldom — or never — gets. Therefore, I appreciate it the more highly." After apologizing for being unable to accept past invitations to attend their functions in other cities, he thanked them for taking the time to "come to the Little White House in Key West and present me with this Scroll, which I shall treasure all my life, and which I shall have in a place of honor in my home when I have a chance to own one."[41]

(Above) President Truman accepting congratulations after being made a life member and past grand master of the Florida Masons by Anthony W. Connor, grand master of Florida, on December 3, 1949. *(U.S. Navy/Harry S. Truman Library)* (Below) President Truman's Masonic dues card. *(Harry S. Truman Library)*

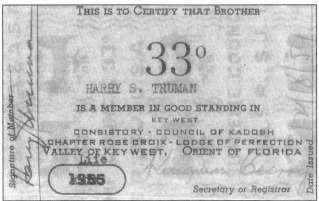

Following the Masonic presentation, Truman was presented with an honorary life membership in the Mahi Temple of the Shrine in Miami, Florida, by Potentate B.H. Blakey of Miami (center). Shaking the president's hand is Shriner and Mayor of Key West Maitland Adams.[42] *(U.S. Navy/Harry S. Truman Library)*

DATE *8 Nov.* 194*8*

The Key West Yacht Club

Takes Pleasure In Tendering To

MR. *Harry S. Truman*

ADDRESS *"The White House"*

This Membership Card, - *Life*

SECRETARY

President Truman was also provided with a life membership in the Key West Yacht Club. *(Harry S. Truman Library)*

The honors kept coming even after Truman left office. During his 1957 post-presidential visit, he was named honorary chairman of the Monroe County Commission. The former president had experience in the parochial nature of county politics as his first elective office was that of administrative judge in Missouri, a position similar to that of county commissioner.

The former president wields the gavel at a Monroe County Commission meeting in 1957. From left: Chairman Gerald Saunders, Commissioner Joe Allen, Harry Truman and Commissioner Harry Harris. *(Monroe County Public Library)*

The honors Truman received in Key West were not just formal ones. Eager to make their famous guest feel welcome, ordinary Key West residents reached out with small, simple and thoughtful gestures.

As a member of the first liaison committee set up to handle all communications between the city and the White House, Paul Sher recalled being kept busy finding items requested by the White House, and handling all the gifts locals wanted to give the president. Years later, his taste buds still remembered a frequent occurrence: "The old ladies at the time were making puddings and cakes and everything else. I got plenty of puddings and cakes in those days — they never got to the White House!"[43]

Very often, island resourcefulness came in handy when it came to fulfilling some of the requests. Finding a 14-karat gold dolphin tie bar for the submarine base commander to present to President Truman in commemoration of his submarine dive on November 21, 1946, was one of those occasions for Paul Sher.

As a jeweler, he knew it would take days to find such an item on the mainland and have it sent to Key West. In order to get the job done, "I stayed up all night and I made them. I got myself a blow torch, took some wedding rings, I melted down the wedding rings and I made a little small cast, poured the gold into it. (The result): Solid gold dolphins."[44]

President Truman showing off the double dolphin tie clasp made by Paul Sher. *(U.S. Navy/Little White House Museum)*

Wesley Saunders remembers the many officers' wives who were eager to make Truman feel comfortable while in Key West. During the first presidential visits, prior to the remodeling of the Little White House in 1949, the Navy wives were concerned that the house, devoid of personal touches, was too bare for the commander in chief. "The ladies," recounts Mr. Saunders, "would gather up bric-a-brac and make it homey." His mother's contribution to the effort was a silver coffee service that she would take over prior to the arrival of the president.[45]

Longtime resident Anna Weekley, whose father founded one of Key West's best known local groceries, Fausto's Food Palace, recalls the challenges of filling the White House grocery list. Some of the requested items, such as canned vichyssoise, were a novelty in tropical Key West, and were not regularly found on Fausto's shelves. When the request first came in for vichyssoise, Mrs. Weekley had not heard of it, but "from then on out we made sure we had plenty on hand."[46]

The thoughtfulness of the island residents towards the president and his family continued long after he left office. Kermit Lewin, mayor of Key West from 1963 to 1969, recalls a nostalgic and generous gesture on the part of the owners of Key West Handprint Fabrics, famous for the unique tropical fabric printed in their local factory. Remembering how Truman and his party had so enjoyed wearing bright, tropical shirts while in Key West during the presidential years, they wanted to be sure the Truman family, visiting on one of the post-presidential trips, had the favored Key West uniform. Knowing that Mayor Lewin would be meeting the former president, they gave him a "bundle of clothes" from Key West Handprint as a gift for the entire Truman family. Mr. Lewin remembers the delighted Mrs. Truman and Margaret playfully arguing over some of them![47]

Locals who spent time with Truman also remember his famous "salty" side. Kermit Lewin dined with the Trumans on several occasions during their post-presidential visits, and remembers one particular dinner at the Little White House as a guest of the base commander.

As was the custom in those days, after having dinner in the dining room, the women retired to another room while the men gathered in the congeniality of the living room to talk. According to Mr. Lewin, Harry Truman was quite a storyteller, and on that particular night his favorite topic was Eisenhower, for whom he still felt the well-documented bitterness stemming from political decisions made by Eisenhower as a Republican candidate during the 1952 campaign.

During this contentious time in their relationship, Eisenhower had made statements signaling "his friendship with Truman was expendable." By these actions, Truman believed "Eisenhower had shown disrespect for the presidency of the United States." [48]

The Eisenhower story told by Truman at the dinner party and remembered by Mayor Lewin was about the day the press came to him asking what he thought of Mr. Eisenhower's announcement that he would not wear the customary top hat to his inaugural. Truman seemed delighted in recounting his reply to the surprised reporters: "I don't care if his ass hangs out."[49]

The story of Truman in Key West would not be complete without some mention of a favorite pastime: poker playing at the poker table on the south porch of the Little White House.

When questioned about those games, former staff members Milton Kayle, Ken Hechler and George Elsey collectively offered their view of the atmosphere surrounding the poker playing. According to them, the game was open to any presidential staff members who wanted to join. Junior or senior, all were equal. Truman played for the fun of it, enjoying the camaraderie and the bantering, and did not know or care what his winnings were.[50]

Locals were also invited to play. Paul Sher played once, remembering it was "a lot of fun, but you were never going to beat him (Truman), and you folded with whatever God gave you." Playing poker with such an important person was uncharted ground for the island merchant as "he would bluff on anything and nobody would call him. After all, he was the President of the United States!" Sher also recalled there being a limit to the game.[51]

The former aides explained the limit this way: "There was a $100 ceiling. If luck was bad and someone went broke, Vaughn (presidential military aide Major General Harry H. Vaughn) would bail him out. Vaughn would 'pinch' the pot every once in awhile and build up the bank which he used to bail out whoever was broke."[52]

The congenial days at the Little White House in Key West came to an abrupt end in 1952 with Truman's decision not to run for a second full term. For Key West, this meant the end of its time in the international spotlight as a presidential retreat. The townspeople, accustomed to the activity and excitement brought about by the visits, were devastated. The local economy suffered. The loss of business was so noticeable that in 1954 the Key West Chamber of Commerce pleaded with former President Truman to move to the island permanently or at least vacation here again.[53]

The reaction of Marlene Carbonell to the news reflects what the entire community felt. She recalls that, as a naïve fifth grader, she had assumed the only president she had ever known would be president forever. When she learned Truman would not be seeking re-election, she was brokenhearted to think not only would he no longer be president, but worse, in her mind, would not be returning to Key West. Gone would be the excitement of knowing that this famous man was in town. Gone would be the pride of standing in front of the Truman School to welcome him back.

She sprang into action. Using her father's typewriter and stationery, she hunted and pecked her way through a letter begging the president to reconsider his decision. Since no one knew what Marlene had done, her father was surprised one day to receive an envelope from the White House addressed to his daughter. The letter from President Truman gave the young girl a civic lesson on presidential tenure, explaining that he had served his time.[54]

Mr. Truman did return periodically as a private citizen, but he never lingered. His return visits to Key West after leaving the White House can be attributed to the special relationship he had with local residents John and Mary Spottswood. The story of the friendship between the descendant of Walter C. Maloney, one of the island's first pioneers who settled in Key West in 1820, and the President of the United States is a unique one.

It began, speculated Paul Sher, because "Jack had the only Cadillac convertible in town. There was no other one in the city of Key West. Every time he (Truman) was coming down, they'd call him (Spottswood)." According to Sher, the local businessman, property owner, radio and cable station owner, one-time Monroe County sheriff, and Florida state senator was a good person to know. "Jack had some connections up on the mainland and was able to get anything they (the White House) wanted."[55]

One of the most publicized examples of the countless ways in which the local businessman was able to facilitate matters for the president and the White House was the great lengths to which he went, as the young 26-year-old owner of Key West's first radio station, to arrange for Truman to hear the March 1947 operatic debut of his daughter, Margaret.

While having the only car in town suitable for presidential transportation may have initiated the introduction, the radio incident certainly solidified the relationship. Through time and circumstance, a twenty-five-year friendship developed between the two men.

To understand the enduring nature of this friendship is to know that, as a fifth-generation Conch closely tied to his community, John Spottswood fully appreciated the economic and political ramifications the selection of Key West as a presidential retreat could have on his remote hometown. He genuinely wanted this important guest to like Key West and to return.

As explained by his eldest son, Jack Spottswood, "He felt we never had the population base to be powerful enough politically to make an impact on the state or national level. He cultivated back door channels with people in power to get things done for Key West." To that end, he devoted time, energy and personal resources not just to President Truman, but in later years, to many national and state figures. He did so, "not for himself, but for the community."[56]

His motivation, however, was often misunderstood, causing long-term repercussions and leading him to once comment: "The mistake I made was making my community my hobby."[57] However, according to his son, despite the speculation surrounding his motives, John Spottswood was driven simply by the desire to keep the president coming to Key West, not by trying to position or promote himself. His son believes the perceptive president recognized this and "that is how the connection was made."[58]

Over time a relationship of trust was built between President Truman and the Key West Conch, lasting well beyond his White House years. When Truman's presidential tenure was over, it was John Spottswood and his wife, Mary, who invited Truman and his family for their numerous return visits to Key West, graciously offering to have them stay in their home or at their various resort properties.

Because Truman "respects the office, both in and out of office,"[59] it can be said it was the friendship between the two families, rather than a sense of entitlement, that led the former president and his family to accept the Spottswoods' invitations to vacation in Key West following his departure from the White House.

The younger Spottswood's memories of the family's presidential guest provide insight into the respect his father had for the president and the trust Truman had in his Key West friend. He recalls the protective role assumed by his father as he accompanied the former president on his visits to Key West, throughout the Florida Keys, and sometimes to Miami. During those travels, John Spottswood would not let people they met initiate discussions about serious issues unless Truman asked to do so. Knowing that he would thus be shielded allowed Truman to let his guard down and relax.[60]

Former President Harry Truman with state senator John Spottswood (left) and Florida Governor Ferris Bryant (right). Truman often crossed his arms for photographs as he maintained that the "SOBs are always cutting people out of my photos."[61] *(Courtesy Spottswood Family Collection)*

Yet another gesture illustrates John Spottswood's ability to balance Truman's desire not to receive special privileges after leaving office with his own respect for the former president and for the stature of the office of the presidency. At his own expense, Spottswood purchased a 1957 Cadillac limousine for the use of the Truman family during their post-presidential visits. As Truman was no longer authorized to use the presidential seal, his special status was subtly acknowledged in the simple initials HST on the vanity plates Spottswood had placed on the car's front bumper.

John Spottswood's 1957 Cadillac limousine sporting the HST vanity plate. *(Little White House Museum)*

President Truman relaxing with, seated from left, Judge Samuel Rosenman of New York, Bess Truman and Mary Spottswood on the Spottswoods' private island retreat, Munson Island, now Little Palm Island Resort. *(U. S. Navy/Harry S. Truman Library)*

Former President Harry Truman and Senator John Spottswood aboard Spottswood's boat in the Florida Keys in 1964. *(Ed Swift, Jr./ Little White House Museum)*

The long-term association between the two men naturally translated into opportunities for John Spottswood and his family. Truman arranged to have his Key West friend appointed a sergeant at arms at the 1948 Democratic National Convention. On a later trip to Miami with the former president, during which Truman was made honorary rabbi by the Miami Jewish community in honor of his strong support for the independent state of Israel, John Spottswood was similarly honored.[62]

The friendship extended to the entire Spottswood family. Second son Robert traveled to Cape Canaveral with the former president and his grandchildren for a tour of the space facility. In 1968, college freshman Jack Spottswood was given a ride back to school aboard the presidential plane. He recalls now that at the time he exhibited typical eighteen-year-old nonchalance. Upon learning that the route to Tulane went through Kansas City, he needed to be reminded by his father that the privilege of this unique experience far outweighed the circuitous route. On the flight, young Jack and the former president engaged in comfortable small talk. Only upon landing in Kansas City, as he watched Truman being greeted by a large entourage, did the realization of the enormous stature of the family friend finally set in.[63]

Harry and Bess Truman and John and Mary Spottswood in the living room at the Little White House as guests of Commander McCorkle during a post-presidential visit in 1957. *(Little White House Museum)*

President Truman with the children of John and Mary Spottswood, Robert, Bill, Jack and Farnie, in 1960 on the porch of 531 Caroline Street, the Spottswood family home. *(Courtesy Spottswood Family Collection)*

By his actions, John Spottswood appeared to prefer not to call attention to his friendship with Truman. Local woodcarver, Frank Balbontin tells a story illustrating his self-effacing attitude. Spottswood had commissioned Balbontin to create one of his primitive woodcut paintings as a gift for the president. Upon viewing the work prior to its presentation, John Spottswood saw something he did not like. In the work, a scene depicting Truman on the lawn in front of the Little White House, was an image of himself standing next to the president. He insisted that he be removed from the piece. Working in acrylics, Balbontin was able to quickly comply.[64]

A duplicate by Frank Balbontin of his original woodcarving is on display in the exhibit rooms at the Little White House Museum. *(Little White House Museum)*

President Harry S. Truman died on December 26, 1972. A state funeral was held on December 28, 1972, on the grounds of the Harry S. Truman Library in Independence, Missouri, where he is buried.

On that same day in Key West, local citizens gathered at Truman Beach for their own special memorial service. Key West Mayor Charles (Sonny) McCoy and Rear Admiral John Maurer, commander of the Key West Naval Station, placed a wreath in the waters of the Gulf of Mexico in memory of the former president who had brought so much attention to the island city. Senator Spottswood spoke to the true reason the man from Missouri felt a special bond with Key West, "President Truman was as close to an ordinary citizen as he could be here."[65]

A wreath in memory of President Truman was placed by the Navy on the presidential gates leading to the Little White House. *(U.S. Navy/Harry S. Truman Library)*

Key West's high regard for this president is expressed in a permanent and uniquely Key West manner: a bronze bust of Harry S. Truman stands on a natural keystone pedestal in the shady Key West Memorial Sculpture Garden in the heart of Old Town, within walking distance of the Little White House.

This simple memorial to Truman is in the company of the men and women, most relatively unknown outside of Key West, who contributed significantly, and sometimes colorfully, to the history of the island community.

The inclusion of Harry Truman in the Key West Memorial Sculpture Garden is a tribute not only to his contributions to the country and the world, but to the impact he had on the city and the people of Key West. Perhaps more importantly, the somewhat guarded and normally insular Conchs proudly consider him one of their own.

Made possible by the generosity of the Shannon Foundation, this bust of President Harry S. Truman stands in the Key West Memorial Sculpture Garden. *(Courtesy Key West Memorial Sculpture Garden Foundation)*

The story of Truman in Key West is now told at the Little White House Museum through its permanent exhibits and informed tour guides, themselves students of Truman history. It is there that the legacy of America's 33rd president and his presence in Key West is relived each day.

CHAPTER FIVE

Visitors Past and Present
The Little White House Legacy

While President Truman is most closely associated with the Little White House and Key West, many other presidents, politicians and dignitaries have visited Key West, and many have stayed in the Little White House. This setting appeared to provide an intangible atmosphere which was beneficial to solving the problems at hand. This list of visitors is notable.

PRESIDENT ULYSSES S. GRANT

Ulysses S. Grant was the first of many presidents to visit the small island of Key West. In 1881, before Quarters A was built and when the only access to Key West was by boat, President Grant, traveling with General Phil Sheridan, stopped briefly in Key West while on a world cruise and lecture tour.

The citizens of Key West turned out to welcome Grant during a parade down Duval Street. *(National Archives/Wright Langley)*

155

PRESIDENT WILLIAM HOWARD TAFT

The train brought President William Howard Taft to Key West on December 12, 1912. His trip by rail down the Florida Keys was made possible by the completion of the "railroad that went to sea." Just eleven months earlier, on January 22, 1912, this incredible engineering feat, often called the Eighth Wonder of the World, connected the Florida Keys to the U. S. mainland.

The grueling task of building a railroad that spanned the 120 miles of islands and waters of the Florida Keys was accomplished through the ingenuity and perseverance of Henry Morrison Flagler. His vision was to connect his rail line to the ships coming through the Panama Canal, which was then under construction. He gambled that after leaving the Panama Canal the ships would sail though the Straits of Florida and their cargo could then be off-loaded in Key West to be placed in his rail cars for the trip up the east coast.[1]

At the reception for President Grant, the menu included such delicacies as beef tongue, pickled turtle, walnut ketchup and vanilla ice cream. *(Monroe County Public Library)*

President Taft followed the route Flagler hoped others would follow. After visiting with Key West Mayor J. N. Fogarty, President Taft and his party boarded the presidential yacht, the USS *Arkansas,* and sailed to Panama to inspect construction of the Panama Canal.[2]

12/21/12 Key West

Pres. Taft at Mayor Fogarty's

(Left) The home of Mayor and Mrs. J.N. Fogarty on the corner of Duval Street and Caroline Street, decorated in honor of the visit of President William H. Taft on December 21, 1912. *(Monroe County Public Library)* (Below) President Taft, with Mayor Fogarty on his right, leaving the Fogarty home. *(Monroe County Public Library)*

President William Howard Taft, sixth from the left in the front row, and his party preparing to board the USS *Arkansas*, moored behind Base Commander Lucian Young's Quarters A home. *(Monroe County Public Library)*

THOMAS EDISON

While in Key West for six months in 1918 working on his Edison batteries that were used to power the U.S. submarines, Thomas Edison resided in Quarters A, which was at that time converted into a roomy single-family home. He stayed as the guest of the base commander, whose wife "often decorated Edison's room with bougainvillaea flowers, a homey touch said to please him."[3]

Edison was so engrossed in his work in Key West that he was unable to attend the wedding of his son, Charles Edison, across the state in Fort Myers. In declining the invitation Edison wrote, "If you have decided it must be, then the sooner it is done the better. It can't be worse than life in the front line trenches. Impossible for Theodore or myself to come."[4]

Thomas Edison standing in front of the underwater explosives used as anti-submarine mines he perfected during his stay in Key West. (*National Archives/Monroe County Public Library*)

PRESIDENT CALVIN COOLIDGE

President Calvin Coolidge also followed the route of Flagler's grand design. In 1928, after participating in a Pan American conference held in Havana, Cuba, he and Mrs. Coolidge sailed on the USS *Memphis* to Key West and returned to Washington, D.C., via Flagler's railroad. Key West Mayor Leslie Curry insisted that the First Family see Key West before their departure.[5]

(Above) President and Mrs. Coolidge arriving in Key West aboard the USS *Memphis*. *(Courtesy Gregory Curry)* (Below left) President and Mrs. Coolidge with Key West Mayor Leslie Curry. *(Courtesy Gregory Curry)* (Below right) President and Mrs. Coolidge departing Key West via Flagler's East Coast Railway. *(National Archives/Monroe County Public Library)*

PRESIDENT FRANKLIN D. ROOSEVELT

The hurricane on Labor Day 1935 destroyed Flagler's Florida East Coast Railway, and with it Key West lost its land link to the Florida mainland. Once again the island community was isolated.

Following the devastation, the railroad was not rebuilt as it had not developed into the successful trade route Flagler had envisioned. The train's right of way was acquired by the United States government, over which it constructed the Overseas Highway, U.S. Route 1.

In February 1939, President Franklin D. Roosevelt arrived in Key West, after having driven down the Keys from Miami in an open convertible inspecting the new highway, which had officially opened on July 4, 1938.

President Roosevelt on the new U. S. Highway 1 on Feb. 19, 1939. Bahia Honda Bridge is in the background. (L to R) Mr. Smith; Miami attorney Paul Marks; Overseas Road Commission Chairman John Slade, Sr.; Key West Mayor Willard Albury; Bridge Commissioner John Costar, Sr.;Miami Mayor Alex Orr; Monroe County Commissioner C.C. Symonettee and former Miami Mayor Ed Sewell.*(Monroe County Public Library)*

President Roosevelt officially opened the 1939 Golden Gate Exposition in San Francisco via radio address from Key West. This address was delivered outdoors at the Greene Street gate to the Naval Station, just one block from Quarters A. President Roosevelt, Admiral William Leahy and Key West Mayor Willard Albury are seen here at the Greene Street naval gate as Roosevelt delivers the radio address. *(Monroe County Public Library)*

Following the ceremonies Roosevelt "remained in Key West to relax and fish. The city's gratitude for the aid of his FERA, WPA, and PWA was expressed by the most enthusiastic parade the community had ever seen. Key Westers named for him the beautiful boulevard which dramatically rims most of the island waterfront."[6]

SECRETARY OF DEFENSE JAMES FORRESTAL AND THE JOINT CHIEFS OF STAFF

In an effort to restructure and rebuild the armed forces following World War II, the National Security Act of 1947 was passed. However, the inability to work out the details to implement the law caused such tension and paralysis among the branches of the armed services that for four days in March 1948, Secretary of Defense James Forrestal "summoned the Joint Chiefs (Leahy, Bradley, Denfield and Spaats) and their aides, in the seclusion of the Key West Naval Base." There they attempted "to grapple with the paralyzing divisions between the Services and to reform the Military Establishment as a whole into a genuinely integrated team, designed to meet the actual rather that the theoretic military problems confronting the country."[7]

This meeting, held in the relaxed atmosphere of the Little White House, resulted in some compromise. The Joint Chiefs arrived at "broad and basic decisions,"[8] and drafted the "Key West Agreement," which spelled out details of the roles and missions of the branches of services. However, once they were back in Washington, the fractiousness continued.[9]

GENERAL DWIGHT D. EISENHOWER

On March 21, 1949, General Eisenhower experienced severe intestinal problems requiring hospitalization. "Truman told Eisenhower that Florida sunshine would be the best medicine for a swift recovery. The president made available the Little White House at Key West and had Eisenhower flown south on the new presidential airplane, *Independence*."[10]

Eisenhower's illness may have been attributable, in part, to ongoing "bickering between the services,"[11] in their attempt to agree to the details of the broader mandate of the National Security Act of 1947 to unify the armed forces as equal members of the National Security Establishment.[12]   In the absence of agreement of the details, "no intelligent division of military manpower, munitions or money could be made.[13]

Once Eisenhower had sufficiently recovered from his illness, the latter part of his fifteen-day stay at the Little White House was spent brokering a lasting agreement among the Joint Chiefs.   In his new role as presiding officer of the Joint Chiefs, Eisenhower met with them at the Little White House in April 1949. Louis Johnson presided as Secretary of Defense, having been sworn in on March 28, 1949, following the resignation of James Forrestal.[14]

The meetings were fraught with frustration. Eisenhower noted in his diary, "The situation grows intolerable. (Admiral) Denfield apparently wants to do right, but he practically retires from every discussion in favor of (Vice Admiral Arthur) Struble, who infuriates everyone with his high, strident voice and apparent inability to see any view point except his own."[15]

Although contentious, progress was made. On August 10, 1949, President Truman signed the National Security Act amendment creating the Department of Defense, with the army, navy and air force as members. The law also provided for a permanent chairman of the Joint Chiefs of Staff.[16]   Truman credited Eisenhower for the success: "The Chiefs have made outstanding progress since you became their presiding officer."[17]

(Above) General Eisenhower meeting on the Little White House lawn with the Joint Chiefs and their aides on April 13, 1949. *(U. S. Navy/Dwight David Eisenhower Library)* (Below) Seated: General Eisenhower; standing from left: Admiral Louis E. Denfield, General Omar Bradley (who later became the first chairman of the Joint Chiefs) and General Hoyt S. Vandenberg on April 13, 1949. *(Monroe County Public Library)*

EISENHOWER'S PRESIDENTIAL VISITS

In September 1955, Dwight David Eisenhower, then President of the United States, suffered a heart attack. In the fall, during his recovery at his Gettysburg, Pennsylvania farm his doctor, General Howard Snyder, stressed the need for an extended period of relaxation so the president could properly heal. Eisenhower considered a vacation at his retreat on the Augusta National Golf Course, but the warmer Key West was suggested as a more suitable location for outdoor walking.[18]

The Florida press jumped on the public relations bandwagon: "In choosing Key West over Augusta for his continued convalescence, Mr. Eisenhower demonstrated again the sound judgment which has made him a popular President. His selection was, after all, largely a matter of arithmetic. He looked at the Augusta temperatures: 43 to 51. Then he looked at Key West temperatures: 68 to 77. Quick subtraction showed it was 25 degrees warmer in Florida – warm enough for outdoor putting and sunbathing."[19]

Upon hearing the radio announcement of the plans for the president to take a southern vacation, numerous other locations, and even private homes, were offered to him and his party for their use.[20] Much to the delight of Key West residents, Key West was chosen, and President Eisenhower arrived in Key West the last week of December 1955.

The Little White House was unavailable for Eisenhower's use, having been converted back into a duplex following President Truman's departure from office. Its occupants were Rear Admiral George Tower, the base commander, and Lt. Commander Sid Chapman. President Eisenhower, Mrs. Eisenhower and her mother, Mrs. John Doud, resided in Quarters L, just down the street from Truman's Little White House.[21]

(Above) Eisenhower's motorcade into Key West followed the same route as Truman had used, each step along the way bearing reminders of past presidential visitors. From Boca Chica, Eisenhower traveled along Roosevelt Boulevard, down Truman Avenue and past the Margaret-Truman Launderette at the corner of Truman Avenue and Margaret Street. In keeping with tradition, Key West officials named a street Eisenhower Drive. *(Florida Natural Color, Inc./Little White House Museum)* (Below) President and Mrs. Eisenhower leaving Quarters L on December 29, 1955. *(Dwight David Eisenhower Library)*

Key West citizens showed their pleasure in having another presidential guest by inviting President Eisenhower and his party to social events. However, his appointments were limited to "those matters of an urgent and official nature so that he can have as much rest and relaxation as possible."[22]

Once again, Paul Sher's resourcefulness was needed to fulfill some requests of the presidential party. He recalled, "The lady (Mrs. Eisenhower) wanted pink gooseneck lamps for her bedroom and you know there is no such animal in Key West. So I went out to Peggy Mills' furniture store, found some green ones and painted them pink!"[23]

The next thing they wanted were finger bowls, quite foreign to the more relaxed Key West social circles. Fortunately for Sher, he remembered an item he had purchased for a promotion in his jewelry store on Duval Street: a small glass mayonnaise bowl. Minus its saucer and spoon, it proved to be a suitable substitute, and luckily he had twenty-four![24]

Although the primary objective of the visit was recuperative, President Eisenhower did take time to meet with various national and international visitors, again thrusting Key West into the world's spotlight.

The Naval Station Administration Building across from the Little White House was used by President Eisenhower on January 8, 1956, to hold a press conference dealing with the 1956 State of the Union Address.[25] *(U. S. Navy/Dwight David Eisenhower Library)*

(Above) President Eisenhower and Brazilian President-elect Juscelino Kubitschek leaving Quarters L following a meeting on January 5, 1956. *(U. S. Navy/Dwight David Eisenhower Library)* (Below)President Eisenhower greeting General Al Gruenther, former head of the North Atlantic Treaty Organization, during his visit to Key West on January 5, 1956. On the right is the president's brother, Milton Eisenhower. *(U. S. Navy/Dwight David Eisenhower Library)*

President Eisenhower leaving the Little White House grounds on December 30, 1955, followed by Dr. Milton Eisenhower, Dr. Howard Snyder, Press Secretary James Hagerty, and members of the press. *(Little White House Museum)*

The Key West presidential prescription, first tried by President Truman in 1946, had positive results for Eisenhower as well. According to James C. Hagerty, Eisenhower's press secretary, "I personally think Dr. Snyder thinks the sun here has done the President a world of good. He has been able to get his work done, get exercise and to relax here at Key West."[26] He also enjoyed a ball game between the press corps and the Secret Service agents, tried his hand at deep-sea fishing, practiced his golf shots and worked on two paintings, one of a Colorado mountain and a Key West scene.[27]

On January 3, 1956, the Monroe County Board of Commissioners passed a resolution welcoming President Eisenhower, and expressed "the fervent hope and prayer that the recuperative powers of our health giving sunshine, of which the Almighty has endowed us in abundance, may have the desired effect of hastening his complete recovery."[28]

With memories still fresh of the economic advantages of hosting a presidential guest, the county commissioners opportunistically seized the moment to promote Key West: "We trust that he will honor us again and again in the future by returning to relax and rest in our peaceful, tropical atmosphere."[29]

JOHN FOSTER DULLES

The recuperative powers of Key West's "health giving sunshine" became well known in Washington circles. Secretary of State John Foster Dulles visited Key West from November 16 to December 3, 1956, to enjoy the warm weather as he recovered from stomach cancer.[30] He stayed at Casa Alante, next to the naval hospital, and on November 27, 1956, received a visit from Vice President Richard Nixon, who was vacationing in Miami at the time.[31]

Secretary of State John Foster Dulles, with Vice President Richard Nixon on right and John Spottswood on left, in Key West on November 27, 1956. *(Wright Langley/Little White House Museum)*

During the Dulles visit an inadvertent eavesdropping incident brought hope that Key West might again become a presidential retreat. While routinely checking government-assigned telephone cables, Key West resident Harry Knight, then local manager of American Telephone and Telegraph, accidentally cut into a conversation between Dulles in Key West and President Eisenhower in Augusta, Georgia.

Fearing that the distinct disconnecting click would be noticed by both parties, Harry Knight stayed on the line. What he heard prompted him to take action. Ike was complaining about the rainy weather in Augusta; Dulles countered with the suggestion that Ike move down to Key West. Eisenhower's reply grabbed Knight's attention: He could not vacation in Key West because it only had a nine-hole golf course.

At the end of the conversation, Knight called the chamber of commerce with the news that Key West might get Eisenhower to visit regularly if it had an eighteen-hole course. The city hired Rees Jones to design an eighteen-hole championship course. The golf course was built, but it was not enough to lure Eisenhower away from Augusta.[32]

PRESIDENT JOHN F. KENNEDY
March 26, 1961

The geopolitical climate of March 1961 brought yet another presidential visit to Key West, and with it came much sought-after international attention. This time, the visitor was President John F. Kennedy.

At the time, President Kennedy was vacationing with family in West Palm Beach, Florida; Britain's Prime Minister Harold Macmillan was visiting Trinidad. On March 26, 1961, they came together in Key West for a one-day summit held at the Naval Administration Building and the Little White House. According to Press Secretary Pierre Salinger, the summit was called to address the development of a serious crisis in Laos. The meetings resulted in a joint communiqué requesting an end to warfare in that country.[33]

President Kennedy arriving at Boca Chica Naval Air Station on March 26, 1961. *(John F. Kennedy Library)*

(Above left) President Kennedy and Prime Minister Macmillan reviewing the troops at Boca Chica on March 26, 1961. *(John F. Kennedy Library)* (Above right) President Kennedy and Prime Minister Macmillan leaving Boca Chica Air Base for the motorcade into Key West on March 26, 1961. *(John F. Kennedy Library)* (Below) Kennedy and Macmillan meeting in the Naval Administration Building. *(John F. Kennedy Library)*

Kennedy and Macmillan approaching the Little White House. *(John F. Kennedy Library)*

PRESIDENT JOHN F. KENNEDY
November 26, 1962

The effects of the Cuban Missile Crisis on Key West brought President Kennedy back to the island city a second time.

The proximity of Key West to Cuba placed the island in the center of the escalating tensions between the United States and the Soviet Union. These tensions were precipitated by the sovietization of Cuba, a mere 90 miles away, and furthered in September 1962 by the discovery on Cuba of the installation of one 134 Soviet SS4 missiles, each with a striking range of 2,000 miles. In keeping with the Cold War philosophy of containment, they had been placed there by the Soviets as a counter to the Jupiter missiles placed in Turkey by the United States and its NATO allies.[34]

Key West prepared for a possible invasion by Cuban forces. Barbed wire was strung along the entire length of George Smathers Beach on the Atlantic side of the island. Hawk missile sites, readied to shoot down Soviet aircraft, were installed in the Salt Ponds next to Key West International Airport, on the beach, and up in the Keys.[35]

Following a series of armed escalations on both sides, the world was closer to nuclear war than ever before. Secretly, Robert Kennedy approached the Soviet ambassador and offered a pledge from the United States not to invade Cuba in exchange for the removal of Soviet missiles and the possibility of the U.S. removal of missiles in Turkey. The Soviets agreed and the war was averted.[36]

Although the nuclear threat was diffused, the Soviet-backed government of Cuba continued to be a perceived threat. Tourists stayed away from Key West, severely hurting the island's economy.

President Kennedy's trip to Key West in November 1962 was made to simultaneously award military decorations and create positive press coverage for South Florida.[37] On this trip he visited the many naval installations in Key West, considerably expanded as a direct response to the Soviet presence in Cuba.

President Kennedy inspecting the Hawk missile sites at the Salt Ponds adjacent to the Key West International Airport on November 26, 1962. *(John F. Kennedy Library)*

(Top) President Kennedy, hatless in back of the convertible, reviewing the Navy sailors "manning the rails" in his honor. *(John F. Kennedy Library)* (Right) President Kennedy, in civilian clothes, walking up the gangway of the destroyer USS *Saufley. (John F. Kennedy Library)*

(Below right) President Kennedy reviewing the Key West naval facility. *(John F. Kennedy Library)* (Below left) President Kennedy leaving from the inspection of a submarine at the Key West Submarine Base. *(John F. Kennedy Library)*

FRANCIS CARDINAL SPELLMAN

On May 15, 1964, His Eminence, Francis Cardinal Spellman, was a guest of Rear Admiral Lewis Kirn at the Little White House. As the military vicar of all American Catholics in the Armed Forces, Cardinal Spellman came to administer the sacrament of confirmation to 80 children and 31 adults.[38]

VICE PRESIDENT HUBERT H. HUMPHREY

Vice President and Mrs. Hubert H. Humphrey visited Key West twice. On November 20-21, 1966, they came to vacation as guests of Rear Admiral T. A. Christopher.

Hubert and Muriel Humphrey took advantage of the great fishing off Key West, fishing from the admiral's boat and catching a sailfish weighing 10 lbs. 12 oz.[39]   *(Wright Langley/ Little White House Museum)*

In July 1967, Vice President Humphrey returned again, this time to dedicate the new Navy desalinization plant. The plant was to be the example for all seacoast towns as the future source of drinking water.[40]

KING HUSSEIN I OF JORDAN

King Hussein I of Jordan made an unpublicized, informal visit to Key West on April 13, 1972, as the guest of the base commander, Rear Admiral John H. Maurer.

(Above) His Majesty King Hussein of Jordan and Rear Admiral John H. Maurer seated on the south porch of the Little White House during the king's visit on April 13, 1972. *(U.S. Navy/Monroe County Public Library)* (Below) His Majesty King Hussein descending the Little White House stairs. *(U. S. Navy/Monroe County Public Library)*

PRESIDENT JIMMY CARTER

December 31, 1996, was a night to remember at the Little White House. Former President Jimmy Carter and Mrs. Carter, along with a number of Carter family members, held a brief family reunion in the Florida Keys. During their visit, Mr. and Mrs. Henry Drettman, whose company at the time managed the Little White House Museum for the state of Florida, hosted a New Year's Eve dinner for the Carter family at the Little White House.

The Carter family dining in the Little White House at the stately Truman dining room table. *(Richard Watherwax/Little White House Museum)*

The Carters with entertainer Bobby Nesbitt at the Truman piano. *(Richard Watherwax/Little White House Museum)*

THE NEW MILLENNIUM
The Legacy Continues

The historic setting of the Little White House, used by so many great leaders in the past, is the perfect setting for the present.

The historic importance of the Little White House, the relaxed atmosphere of the grounds, and the security of its setting continue to be recognized on a national and international level. "Dignified, but warm and friendly" was the description of the ambiance given by a government official upon viewing the site as a place to host government dignitaries.

THE JOINT CHIEFS OF STAFF
CHOD QUAD Meeting

The legacy of the Little White House as a place for the Joint Chiefs of Staff to gather which began during the Truman and Eisenhower eras, was continued by General Henry H. Shelton, Chairman of the Joint Chiefs of Staff of the United States. On March 31, 2000, Shelton selected the historic presidential retreat as the site for a dinner he hosted honoring his military counterparts from Great Britain, Germany and France.

Attending as guests of General and Mrs. Henry Shelton were General Sir Charles Guthrie, Chief of the Defense Staff of the United Kingdom, and Lady Guthrie; General Jean-Pierre Kelche, Chief of the Armed Forces General Staff of France and Mrs. Kelche; and General Hans-Peter Von Kirchbach, Chief of Staff, Federal Armed Forces of Germany. The dinner was the opening event of a biannual series of weekend meetings, regularly held by the generals to keep open the lines of communication among these close allies.

Lt. Colonel Harold Shamblin, Deputy Director of Protocol for the Chairman of the Joint Chiefs of Staff, remarked that the Key West meeting, "was truly a high point for us all and the comments from the generals were glowing. They got a tremendous amount of work done in minimum conference time and had the pleasure of tasting the best of Key West at the same time. The Chairman's comment was that we have set a high water mark for future meetings."[41]

Toasting long-standing friendships are from left, General Sir Charles Guthrie, Mrs. Carolyn Shelton, General Hans-Peter Von Kirchbach, General Henry H. Shelton, General Jean-Pierre Kelche and Lady Kate Guthrie.(*U. S. Department of Defense/Little White House Museum*)

SECRETARY OF STATE COLIN POWELL
THE NOGORNO-KARABAKH PEACE CONFERENCE

Yet another page of Little White House history opened in April 2001 when the United States Department of State selected the site for treaty negotiations between Armenia and Azerbaijan.

These must be considered the highest level of talks, as they were held directly between President Robert Kocharian of Armenia and President Heydar Aliyev of Azerbaijan, with Secretary of State Colin Powell representing the president of the United States. Under the auspices of the Organization for Security and Cooperation in Europe, delegates representing France, Russia and the United States worked with the nations in conflict to try to find a peaceful solution to their long-held differences.

The importance of these peace talks was confirmed by Secretary Powell in a statement he made to the *Key West Citizen*: "A peaceful settlement is key to the future of the South Caucasus. This is one more important step in an ongoing process to find peace for that region."[42]

Secretary of State Colin Powell opening the Key West Peace Talks on April 6, 2001, on the lawn of the Little White House. *(Andy Newman/Little White House Museum)*

United States Chief Negotiator Ambassador Carey Cavanaugh, best described the appropriateness of the Little White House for the meeting: "The garden especially provided a relaxing atmosphere. We then had a good formal meeting in different rooms with the three co-chairs."[43]

The Truman Little White House was once again alive with activity! The many rooms, which for ten years had been lying dormant as if under museum glass, were once again used for high-level meetings.

For their most formal meeting, from which a joint statement to the world was issued, the two presidents, Secretary Powell and the ambassadors gathered in the living room, around President Truman's famous round poker table, with its table-top in place. Its use was a calculated choice, and it was carefully moved from the south porch to the center of the living room to accommodate the formal needs of this important meeting. Truman, who wanted to be remembered for his efforts on world peace, would certainly have been pleased.

Seated around the table from left, President of Azerbaijan, Heydar Aliyev; United States Secretary of State Colin Powell; President of Armenia Robert Kocharian; and United States Special Negotiator Carey Cavanaugh gathered for the formal opening session in the Little White House living room. *(Andy Newman/Little White House Museum)*

Following the initial meeting of the principals, treaty language was discussed throughout the rooms of the house, and side conferences were held. The video room on the second floor became the MAP room, where satellite images were analyzed for the sensitive territory negotiations.

As if guided by President Truman's old schedule, the entire delegation gathered each morning on the south porch for breakfast. Lunch was served at the Little White House each day. The Presidents then spent the afternoons resting or enjoying being Key West tourists.

Around 4 p.m. each day, the delegations gathered again at the Little White House to review the staff's accomplishments. Well into the soft tropical Key West night, smaller groups gathered in clusters on the lawns to try to resolve differences.

Secretary of State Colin Powell sharing a light moment with President Heydar Aliyev of Azerbaijan on the lawn of the Little White House on April 6, 2001. *(Andy Newman/Little White House Museum)*

THE TRUMAN LEGACY SYMPOSIUM

As a fitting tribute to the legacy of Harry Truman, a gathering of presidential scholars was held in Key West on June 13-14, 2003. The first of a planned annual event, this symposium focused on Truman's impact on the shape of national security and foreign policy.

The opening reception was held on the Little White House lawns, the site of so many historic meetings and negotiations since the Truman days. Special guests, former Truman aides George Elsey, Milton Kayle and Ken Hechler, took a nostalgic tour of the Little White House, where they had once stayed as part of the White House staff accompanying President Truman on his working vacations.Also present at the symposium was Truman's grandson, Clifton Truman Daniel.

Symposium participants enjoying the opening reception held on the Little White House lawns. (Above left) Former presidential aide Ken Hechler with Truman impersonator Neil Johnson. (Above right) Clifton Truman Daniel, grandson of Harry Truman, acknowledging the crowd. Truman's great-grandson, Wesley Daniel, is seated with his back to the camera, and Ken Hechler is in the background. (Above center) George Elsey, former special assistant to Truman, is seated on the Little White House lawn engaged in conversation with Carol Shaughnessy of the Monroe County Tourist Development Council. *(Little White House Museum)*

The inspiring symposium, held the following day, created in the minds of all those attending an awareness of the enduring national and global legacy of President Truman's foreign policy decisions.

(Above) Three former Truman aides, fielding questions at the 2003 Truman Legacy Symposium held at Florida Keys Community College. From left, George Elsey, Milton Kayle and Ken Hechler. *(Little White House Museum)* (Below left) George Elsey (Below right) Clifton Daniel (Below center) Keynote speaker General Brent Scowcroft, who served as National Security Advisor for Presidents Gerald Ford and George H.W. Bush, with Ken Hechler. *(/Little White House Museum)*

There is a historic continuum to the legacy of Harry Truman's modest Little White House in Key West. That it continues to be selected as the site for meetings of significant national and international proportions is a tribute to both the enduring legacy of President Truman and to the relaxing atmosphere, so conducive to compromise, found in the home and its surroundings.

Remarks made at the conclusion of the Key West Peace Talks on April 10, 2001, by Ambassador Cavanaugh best describe these intangible qualities. In an open letter to the citizens of Key West in the *Key West Citizen*, he commented, "Our discussions there were infused with the spirit of former President Harry S. Truman, who was also tireless in the pursuit of peace." The Little White House staff, he continued, "made Truman's home into our home, allowing us to add a new page of history to its already rich legacy. It was the perfect setting."[44]

Secretary of State Colin Powell seated at President Truman's desk in the living room of the Little White House on April 6, 2001.

Notes

Chapter One: The Sentinel of the Straits

1 Jefferson Browne, *Key West: The Old and the New*, 1912, ed. Bicentennial Floridiana Facsimile Reprint Series (Gainesville, FL: University of Florida Press, 1973)

2 John Viele, *The Florida Keys Volume 2: True Stories of the Perilous Straits*,   (Sarasota, FL: Pineapple Press, Inc., 1999).

3 Walter C. Mahoney, *A Sketch of the History of Key West, Florida*, 1876; ed. Floridiana Facsimile Reprint Series (Gainesville, FL: University of Florida Press, 1968) 8.

4 Browne 70-73.

5 Browne 212.

6 Browne 73.

7 Browne 212.

8 Maloney 9

9 John R. Weaver II, *A Legacy in Brick & Stone – American Defense Forts of the Third System 1816-1867* (Missoula, MT: Pictorial Histories Publishing Co., 2001).

10 Browne 162-166.

11 Monroe County Courthouse, Key West, FL, Office of the Circuit Court, *Monroe County Records Deed Book E*,   539 and Ida Barron Florida Master Site File 8MO244, Application for National Register of Historic Places, 19 July 1973.

12 Maloney 64.

13 *Military Burial Records of the Key West Military*,   Monroe County Public Library Florida History Collection.

14 Browne 74.

15 *Military Burial Records.*

16 Browne 74.

17 Browne 115-124.

18 Captain A. W. Johnson, USN, letter to Rear Admiral E. F. Nichols, USN, 9 August 1883, "U. S. Naval Station Key West 1883," *Florida Keys Sea Heritage Journal* (winter 1999/2000) 12.

19 Lieutenant Commander J. K. Winn, USN, letter to Captain A. W. Johnson, USN, May 1883, "U.S. Naval Station Key West 1883," *Florida Keys Sea Heritage Journal* (winter 1999/2000) 12.

20 Winn to Johnson.

21 Browne 74.

22 Wright Langley, *Key West and the Spanish American War* (Key West, FL: Langley Press, 1998) 37.

23 Langley, 44.

24 Browne 74.

25 DeForest, *Father of Radio: The Autobiography of Lee DeForest* (Chicago: Wilcox & Follett Co., 1950) 173.

26 Browne 75.

27 Winn to Johnson.

28 Clay Blair, Jr., *Silent Victory- The U. S. Submarine War Against Japan* (New York: Lippencott, Williams & Wilkens, 1975) 23.

29 Key West Historical Military Memorial Committee, research for Memorial plaques, Mallory Square, Key West, Florida.

30 Key West Historical Military Memorial Committee.

31 Works Project Administration, Writers Program, *A Guide to Key West*, 2nd Edition (New York: Hastings House, 1949).

32 Key West Historical Military Memorial Committee.

33 Ibid.

34 Key West Rotary Club, Resolution Commending C.E. Reordan, Captain, USN, Key West, June 1946, copy in Little White House Museum Collection.

35 Ibid.

36 Ibid.

37 Margaret Truman, *Harry S. Truman* (New York: William Morrow Co., 1973) 323.

38 Earl Adams, "Truman Discovers Key West by Purpose," *Miami Herald* 7 December 1947: C2.

39 Key West Historical Memorial Committee.

40 Captain Lovelace USN, remarks, Truman Annex Dedication Ceremonies, Key West, 1972.

41 Captain Lawrence S. Cotton, USN, letter to Ed Swift III, 7 February 2003.

42 Ibid.

43 Ibid.

44 Browne 213.

Chapter Two: The Little White House

1 *The Public Papers of the Presidents of the United States*, "Harry S. Truman, 1947" (Washington D. C.: Government Printing Office, 1963) 505.

2 Winn to Johnson 12-13.

3 United States Navy, Bureau of Yards and Docks, *Proposals for the Construction of Two Houses for Officers Quarters at the US Naval Station Key West, Florida,* 14 December 1889.

4 *Proposals for the Construction of Two Houses for Officers Quarters.*

5 United States Navy, Bureau of Yards and Docks, "Contract #141," 31 January 1890.

6 *From Wilderness to Metropolis. The History and Architecture of Dade County (1825-1940)* 2nd ed. (Miami, FL: Metropolitan Dade County Office of Community Development, Historic Preservation Division, 1992) 177.

7 United States Navy, Bureau of Yards and Docks, Lieutenant Commander J. K. Winn, USN, letter to Commodore George B. White, USN, 25 January 1890.

8 United States Navy, Bureau of Yards and Docks, Lieutenant Commander J. K. Winn, USN, letter to Commodore N. H. Farquhar, USN, 3 May 1890.

9 Winn to White. Winn to Farquhar.

10 United States Navy, Bureau of Yards and Docks, Henry R. Smith, P. A. Paymaster, USN, letter to Commodore N. H. Farquhar, USN, 10 April 1890.

11 United States Navy, Bureau of Yards and Docks, Winn, letter to Farquhar, 17 May 1890.

12 United States Navy, Bureau of Yards and Docks, Winn, letter to Farquhar, 24 May 1890.

13 Browne 75.

14 Tom Hambright, Monroe County Public Library, interview with Robert Wolz, 7 January 2002.

15 Earl Adams, "Truman 'Discovered' Key West by Purpose" *Miami Herald*, 7 December 1947: C2.

16 Harry S. Truman letter to Bess Truman, 18 November 1946, *Dear Bess – The Letters from Harry to Bess Truman 1920-1959*, ed. Robert Ferrell (Columbia, MO: University of Missouri Press, 1983) 540.

17 Earl Adams, "Truman Gets Report on Defense Pact," *Miami Herald* 19 Nov. 1948: A1.

18 U. S. Government Manuscript, Harry S. Truman Little White House Museum, *Presidential Trip Log #1, 17-23 November 1948*, ed. William Rigdon.

19 *The Public Papers of the Presidents of the United State*, " Harry Truman 1947," 505.

20 U. S. Government Manuscript, Harry S. Truman Library, *Presidential Trip Log #3, 6-19 March 1949*, ed. William Rigdon.

21 Ferrell, Harry Truman letter to Bess Truman, 28 November 1948.

22 Margaret Truman, *Harry S. Truman* 395.

23 J.H Lasseter, "Proposal for Redecorating Quarters A & B, U. S. Navy Contract Noy 17070," (Miami: Haygood Lasseter Interiors, 1948).

24 J. H. Lasseter, letter to A. C. Husband, Procurement Officer, U. S. Naval Base, Key West, Florida, 20 December 1948.

25 *Presidential Trip Log #3*.

26 Margaret Truman, *Souvenir, Margaret Truman's Own Story* (New York: McGraw-Hill, 1956) 159.

27 United States Navy, Lieutenant Commander K. E. Yedlicka, USN, "Memorandum – Piano, Former President Harry S. Truman," 27 March 1964.

28 U. S. Government Manuscript, Harry S. Truman Library, *Presidential Trip Log #4, 28 November – 20 December 1949*, ed. William Rigdon: 15.

29 "Truman's Poker Table is Relic of Visits," *Key West Citizen*, 28 Dec. 1972.

30 Harry S. Truman, letter to Bess Truman, 6 March 1949, Harry S. Truman Library.

31 Ibid.

32 *New York Times*, 8 March 1949: A1

33 "President Eisenhower's Daily Schedules in Key West," Dwight David Eisenhower Library.

34 U. S. Naval Station Key West, "Quarters A & B Conversion Plan from Duplex to Single Quarters," 26 September 1956.

35 Department of the Navy, "Original Layout Plan Little White House Quarters A Naval Station Key West, Florida," 1972, Harry S. Truman Little White House Museum.

36 Margaret Foresman, City of Key West, letter to Dr. Philip Dobert, Key West Redevelopment Agency, 27 July 1979, City of Key West and Little White House Museum.

37 "A Proposal for the Development of the Little White House, Key West, FL," Concept by Senator Richard Stone and Mayor Charles McCoy, 1976, Little White House Museum.

38 Ibid.

39 "Memorandum of Agreement," 23 March 1986, Agreement between the General Services Administration, The Florida State Preservation Officer and the Council on Historic Preservation, Council of Historic Preservation.

40 Memorandum of Agreement, Item I Restoration, 1.

Chapter Three: The Presidential Visits

1 Harry S. Truman, letter to Ethel Noland, 19 April 1951, *Letters Home by Harry Truman* ed. Monte E. Poen, 2nd ed (Columbia, MO: University of Missouri Press, 1984) 235.

[2] Margaret Truman, *Harry S.Truman* 334.

[3] Margaret Truman, *Harry S. Truman* 335.

[4] Bradford Mobley, *Miami Herald* 7 March 1947.

[5] Commander William M. Rigdon, USN, and James Derieux, *White House Sailor* (Garden City, NY: Doubleday & Co., 1962) 256.

[6] Harry S. Truman, letter to Bess Truman, 18 November 1946, Letter File Pertaining to Family Business and Personal Affairs, Harry S. Truman Library.

[7] Margaret Truman, *Truman* 324.

[8] *Presidential Trip Log #1:* 18.

[9] *Presidential Trip Log #1:* 11-15.

[10] *Presidential Trip Log #1:* 12.

[11] Earl Adams, *Miami Herald* 5 December 1947.

[12] *Presidential Trip Log #1:* 17.

[13] *Key West Citizen* 23 November 1946: 1

[14] Harry S. Truman, "Special Message to the Congress on Greece and Turkey: The Truman Doctrine," 12 March 1947, *Public Papers of the Presidents* (Washington, D.C.:U.S. Government Printing Office, 1963) 178.

[15] Associated Press 7 March 1947.

[16] Associated Press 8 March 1947.

[17] Harry S. Truman, "Special Message to the Congress on Greece and Turkey: The Truman Doctrine."

[18] United Press International 12 March 1947.

[19] Roy Jenkins, *Truman* (New York: Harper & Row Publishers) 102.

[20] Earl Adams, *Miami Herald* 23 March 1947.

[21] *Miami Herald* 13 March 1947.

[22] *Key West Citizen* daily newspapers: 13-19 March 1947.

[23] *Miami Herald* 15 March 1947: 1.

[24] John R. Vosburgh, City Editor, Key West Citizen 5 January 1947.

[25] John Spottswood, Jr., personal interview with Barbara Hayo, 17 July 2003.

[26] Spottswood to Hayo.

[27] Spottswood to Hayo

[28] Wright Langley, speech at Key West Memorial for President Truman, 28 December 1972.

[29] Harry S. Truman, address, "Conservation of the Everglades National Park," 6 December 1947, *Public Papers of the Presidents* (Washington. D. C.: U. S. Government Printing Office, 1963) 506.

[30] *Miami Herald* 6 December 1947: 1.

[31] Harry S. Truman address, "Conservation of the Everglades National Park." 505-508

[32] U.S. Government Manuscripts, Harry S. Truman Library, *Presidential Trip Log #2, 12-19 March 1947*, ed. William Rigdon 16.

[33] *Presidential Trip Log #3.*

[34] Ambassador Warren R. Austin, text of statement, *Discussion of the Palestine Problem in the Security Council*, "The United Nations and Specialized Agencies," Department of State Bulletin. 294.

[35] Austin, statement 294.

[36] U.S. Government Manuscripts, Harry S. Truman Library, *Presidential Trip Log # 4, 20 February- 5 March 1948*, ed. William Rigdon 35.

[37] Austin, statement 294

[38] Ibid.

[39] Austin, statement 295.

[40] *Presidential Trip Log #4:* 42.

[41] U. S. Government Manuscripts, Harry S. Truman Library, *Presidential Trip Log #9,* 2 – 22 March 1951, ed. William Rigdon: 96.

[42] *Presidential Trip Log #4:* 60.

[43] *Tampa Tribune* 2 December 1951: C8.

[44] *Presidential Trip Log #4:* 48.

[45] Harry S. Truman, radio address, *Presidential Trip Log #4:* 51-52.

[46] Harry Truman letter to Bess Truman, 4 March 1948, Letter File Pertaining to Family Business and Personal Affairs, Harry S. Truman Library.

[47] *Presidential Trip Log #4:* 65.

[48] Margaret Truman, *Bess Truman* 395.

[49] Margaret Truman, *Harry S. Truman* 394.

[50] Margaret Truman, *Bess Truman* 304.

[51] U. S. Government Manuscripts, Harry S. Truman Library, *Presidential Presidential Trip Log #7, 28 November- 20 December 1949,* ed. William Rigdon 19-29.

[52] *Presidential Trip Log #7:* 37-38.

[53] Harry S. Truman, transcript of press conference, 20 March 1968, Harry S. Truman Library.

[54] U. S. Government Manuscripts, Harry S. Truman Library, *Presidential Trip Log #5, 7-12 November 1948,* ed. William Rigdon 57.

[55] *Miami Herald* 18 November 1948: A1.

[56] *Miami Herald* 16 November 1948.

[57] *Presidential Trip Log #5* 57.

[58] *Presidential Trip Log #5* 22.

[59] William Hillman, *Mr. President* (New York: Farrar, Straus and Young, 1952) 206-210.

[60] *New York Times* 8 March 1949.

[61] David McCullough, *Truman* (New York: Simon & Schuster, 1992) 887.

[62] U. S. Government Manuscripts, Harry S. Truman Library, *Presidential Trip Log #6, 6-19 March 1949,* ed. William Rigdon 58.

[63] *Presidential Trip Log #6*

[64] Rigdon, *White House Sailor* 257.

[65] *New York Times* 8 March 1949.

[66] K. C. Freuby telegraph to Charlie Ross, 8 March 1949, Papers of Harry Truman, "Records of White House Telegraph Office, Harry S. Truman Library.

[67] Harry S. Truman, letter to Sheriff Walter Clark, Broward County, Florida, 8 December 1949, Harry S. Truman Library.

[68] Rigdon, *White House Sailor* 262.

[69] *Presidential Trip Log #7* 21.

[70] *Presidential Trip Log # 7* 57.

[71] Secretary Vertical File, 20 December 1949, Harry S. Truman Library 7.

[72] Rigdon, *White House Sailor* 262.

[73] Secretary Vertical File, 20 December 1949, Harry S. Truman Library.

[74] David Lawrence, *New York Herald Tribune* 20 March 1950.

[75] U. S. Government Manuscripts, Harry S. Truman, *Presidential Trip Log # 8, 12 March – 10 April, 1950,* ed. William Rigdon 5.

[76] *Key West Outpost* 14 April 1950.

[77] *Presidential Trip Log #8:* 17.

[78] *Presidential Trip Log #8:* 15.

[79] *Presidential Trip Log #8:* 67.

[80] *Key West Citizen* 20 September 1977.

[81] Admiral Robert L. Dennison USN, oral history interview, 6 October 1971, original transcript, Harry S. Truman Library 88-89.

[82] David Lawrence, *New York Herald Tribune* 20 March 1950.

[83] Lawrence, *New York Herald Tribune*.

[84] Lawrence, *New York Herald Tribune*.

[85] Lawrence, *New York Herald Tribune*.

[86] Harry S. Truman letter to Cousin Ralph, 26 March 1950, *Letters Home by Harry Truman*,ed. Monte M. Poen, 2nd ed. (Columbia, MO: University of Missouri Press) 237

[87] Paul G. Pierpaoli, Jr., Truman and Korea – *The Political Culture of the Early Cold War* (Columbia, MO: University of Missouri Press, 1999) 29.

[88] Harry S. Truman, *Memoirs*, 332.

[89] Harry S. Truman, *Memoirs*, Vol. 2 441-442.

[90] U. S. Government Manuscripts, Harry S. Truman Library, *Presidential Trip Log #9, 2 – 22 March 1951*, ed. William Rigdon 13.

[91] Oscar L. Moore, entry to Little White House Museum Journal, 23 February 2003 Little White House Museum, Key West, Florida.

[92] *Presidential Trip Log #9.*

[93] *Presidential Trip Log #9*: 85.

[94] Pierpaoli 50.

[95] *Key West Outpost* 16 March 1951: Vol 5 No4 1.

[96] McCullough 873.

[97] National Archives and Records Service, Joint Chiefs of Staff telegram to Commander in Chief, Far East, Tokyo, Japan, 20 March 1951, Harry S. Truman Library.

[98] William Manchester, *American Caesar, Douglas MacArthur 1880-1964* (Boston: Little Brown & Co., 1978) 388.

[99] Harry S.Truman, *Memoirs*, Vol. 2 441-442.

[100] Manchester 649.

[101] McCollough 855.

[102] U. S. Government Manuscripts, Harry S. Truman Library, *Presidential Trip Log #10, 8 November – 9 December, 1951*, ed. William Rigdon.

[103] *Miami Herald* 20 September 1977.

[104] Harry S. Truman letter to Judge Carl A. Hatch, 29 November 1951, Secretary Vertical Files, Harry S. Truman Library.

[105] Truman to Hatch.

[106] *Miami News* 29 November 1951.

[107] Harry S. Truman letter to E. W. Roberts, 18 August 1948, National Archives and Records Service, Harry S. Truman Library.

[108] Harry S. Truman 1951, Executive Order #10308, "Improving the Means for Obtaining Compliance with the Non Discrimination Provisions of Federal Contracts," *Public Papers of the Presidents* 640.

[109] Kweisi Enfume, forward, *Harry Truman & Civil Rights – Moral Courage & Political Risks* by Michael M. Gardner (Carbondale, IL: Southern Illinois University Press, 2002) xi.

[110] Enfume in Gardner xi

[111] McCullough 873-874..

[112] *New York Herald Tribune* 21 March 1952.

[113] *New York Herald Tribune* 21 March 1952..

[114] *New York Herald Tribune* 21 March 1952.

[115] *New York Herald Tribune* 21 March 1952.

[116] Steve Neal, *Harry & Ike – The Partnership that Remade the Postwar World* (New York: Scribner, 2001) 238.

[117] Bess Truman letter to Mary Spottswood, 5 May 1968, Letter File Pertaining to Family Business and Personal Affairs, Harry S. Truman Library.

[118] *Key West Citizen* 25 February 1960: 10.

[119] *Key West Outpost*: Vol 6 #3.

[120]   United States Navy, Lieutenant Commander K. E. Yedlicka, memorandum to Shop 63, 27 March 1964.

[121] Harry S. Truman, transcript of press conference, 20 March 1968, Key West, Florida, Harry S. Truman Library.

[122] Truman press conference 20 March 1968.

[123] Truman press conference 20 March 1968.

[124] Bess Truman to Mary Spottswood.

Chaper Four: Key West is "Trumanized"

[1] Paul Sher recorded interview with Ed Swift III, 1990, Ed Swift III Key West Oral History Collection.

[2] George Elsey, "Truman and National Security," The Truman Legacy Symposium,   Florida Keys Community College, Key West, 14 June 2003.

[3] Ken Hechler, "Truman and National Security," The Truman Legacy Symposium, Florida Keys Community College, Key West, 14 June 2003.

[4] *Key West Citizen* 18 November 1946: A1.

[5] "Florida Visits By President Tourist Lure," *Miami Herald* 14 Nov. 1948 .

[6] *New York Times*   7 March 1949, Secretary's Files.

[7] *New York Herald Tribune* and *Washington Evening Star*   28 November 1951, Secretary's Files.

[8] *New York Herald Tribune* and *Washington Evening Star*, 28 November 1951.

[9] *Presidential Trip Log # 3*: 5.

[10] Clothing Collection, Harry S. Truman Library.

[11] Rigdon, *White House Sailor* 257.

[12] McCullough, *Truman* 585.

[13] Rigdon, 258.

[14] *Miami Herald*   26 November 1951.

[15] Harry Knight, personal interview with Robert Wolz, 9 April 2003.

[16] Minnie Estevez, personal interview with Ed Swift, 29 April 2003.

[17] U. S. Government Manuscripts, Harry S. Truman Library, *Presidential Trip Log# 11, 7-27 March 1952*, ed. William Rigdon: 59.

[18] Rigdon, 259.

[19] *Presidential Trip Log #6*: 26

[20] *New York Times* and *New York Herald Tribune*, 30 November 1949, Secretary's Files.

[21] Ken Hechler, personal recollection to Barbara Hayo, 13 June 2003.

[22] United Press International 14 November 1951.

[23] Wesley Saunders, telephone interview with Barbara Hayo, 8 April 2003.

[24] Saunders to Hayo

[25] Saunders to Hayo

[26] Saunders to Hayo

[27] Saunders to Hayo

[28] Harry Truman letter to Bess Truman, 21 November 1946, Vertical Letter File Pertaining to Personal Business and Family Matters.

[29] Harry Truman, letter to Bess Truman, 13 March 1949, Vertical Letter File Pertaining to Personal Business and Family Matters.

[30] Donald Cree, written entry into Little White House Museum Journal, 25 February 2002.

[31] Secretary Files: Trip 5: 30 Nov.- 20 Dec. 1948. .

[32] Mary Sweeting and Mary Anne Matchett, personal interview with Robert Wolz, 1 Dec. 1999.

[33] James Calloway, *Miami News* 17 March 1947, Secretary's Files.

[34] Ed Swift III, personal interview with Barbara Hayo, 15 May 2003.

[35] *Key West High School Yearbook*, 1960, vol. 30: 51.

[36] Eugene Roberts, telephone interview with Robert Wolz, 10 January 2003.

[37] Breedlove and Matchett to Wolz.

[38] *Presidential Trip Log #5*: 39.

[39] Merili McCoy, telephone interview with Barbara Hayo, 5 April 2003.

[40] *Presidential Trip Log #5*: 19.

[41] *Presidential Trip Log #7*: 33.

[42] *Presidential Trip Log #7*: 35-37.

[43] Sher to Swift.

[44] Sher to Swift .

[45] Saunders to Hayo.

[46] Ana Weekley, telephone interview with Barbara Hayo, 22 July, 2003.

[47] Kermit Lewin, telephone interview with Barbara Hayo, 27 May 2003.

[48] Steve Neal, 259.

[49] Lewin to Hayo .

[50] George Elsey Ken Hechler and Milton Kayle, round table question and answer session, Truman Legacy Symposium.

[51] Sher to Swift.

[52] Kayle at Truman Legacy Symposium.

[53] "Harry Could Be President of Key West Any Old Day," *Key West Citizen* 1954.

[54] Marlene Carbonell, personal interview with Robert Wolz, February 2000.

[55] Sher to Swift.

[56] Spottswood to Hayo,

[57] Spottswood to Hayo.

[58] Spottswood to Hayo.

[59] "David McCullough on Harry Truman," *Character Above All*, ed. Robert A. Wilson, vol. II, magnetic tape (New York: Simon & Schuster, 1996).

[60] Spottswood to Hayo.

[61] Spottswood to Hayo

[62] Spottswood to Hayo.

[63] Spottswood to Hayo.

[64] Frank Balbontin, personal interview with Robert Wolz, 13 November 2002.

[65] Wright Langley, speech for Truman Key West Memorial Service, 28 December 1972.

Chapter Five: Visitors Past and Present

1 *The Story of a Pioneer, A Brief History of the Florida East Coast Railway* (St. Augustine, Florida: The Record Company)

2 Wright Langley, interview with Robert Wolz, 2 October 1999.

3 Robert Holgrin, Director of Edison home in Ft. Myers, Florida, interview with Robert Wolz, 1 November 1999.

4 Thomas Edison, original handwritten draft of telegram to Charles Edison, 25 March 1918, on exhibit in the Edison–Ford Winter Estate, Ft. Myers, Florida

5 Gregory Curry, grandson of Leslie Curry, interview with Robert Wolz, 12 January 2000.

6 *Miami Daily News*, 18 May 1947: 11.

7 "The March Crisis," *The Forrestal Diaries*, ed. Walter Mills (New York: Viking Press 1951) 390.

8 *The Forrestal Diaries*, 392.

9 Neal, 145-154.

10 Neal, 149-150.

11 McCullough *Truman* 738.

12 Neal, 145-146.

13 *The Forrestal Diaries*, 391.

14 McCullough *Truman* 739.

15 Dwight David Eisenhower, Diary, 19 March 1949 Dwight David Eisenhower Library.

16 Neal, 152.

17 Neal, 152.

18 "For President and Pauper," *Tampa Morning Tribune,* 4 January 1956.

19 "For President and Pauper," *Tampa Morning Tribune*."

20 General Files 9 January 1956, Dwight David Eisenhower Library.

21 *Key West Outpost* 6 January 1956, Monroe County Public Library

22 A.J. Goodpastor letter to Lewis Maxwell, 4 January 1956, Dwight David Eisenhower Library.

23 Sher to Swift

24 Sher to Swift

25 White House Central Files – Southern Trip 28 December 1955 to 8 January 1956, Dwight David Eisenhower Library.

26 *Key West Citizen* 7 January 1956: A1.

27 *Key West Citizen* 31 December 1955: 1.

28 Resolution, Board of County Commissioners of Monroe County, Florida, 3 January 1956, Dwight David Eisenhower Library.

29 Ibid.

30 Tom Hambright, Monroe County Public Library, interview with Robert Wolz, 3 June 2003.

31 *Key West Citizen* 28 November 1956.

32 Harry Knight, personal interview with Robert Wolz, 18 October 2000.

33 Pierre Salinger, press release, 25 March 1961, John F. Kennedy Library.

34 Robert Kennedy, *Thirteen Days* (New York: W.W. Norton & Co. 1969)

35 Hambright to Wolz.

36 Kennedy, *Thirteen Days* 105-110.

37 Hambright to Wolz

38 *Key West Outpost*, 27 March 1964: 1, Monroe County Public Library

39 *Key West Citizen* 22 November 1966.

40 *Key West Citizen* 21 July 1967.

[41] R. Harold Shamblin, Lt. Colonel, USAF, Deputy Director of Protocol, Office of the Chairman, Joint Chiefs of Staff, memorandum for Barbara Hayo, 1 May 2000.

[42] *Key West Citizen* 4 April 2001: A12

[43] *Key West Citizen* 4 April 2001: A1

[44] *Key West Citizen* 11 April 2001: A1